FIRE AND ICE

Cayenne pepper is an enigma—it can burn the tongue but cool the body, promote blood circulation but stop hemorrhaging. Its anti-inflammatory action can reduce the pain and swelling of arthritis; it lowers cholesterol and triglyceride levels for heart health, and fights bacteria and viruses with its high vitamin C content. This extraordinary therapeutic herb, used by healers for thousands of years, can fortify your health armory against a multitude of ills.

ABOUT THE AUTHOR

John Heinerman, Ph.D. has written 38 books on herbal folk medicine, nutrition, diet, and general health. He has given over 1,000 seminars, workshops, and convention lectures throughout North America. Dr. Heinerman has done extensive research in medical and nutritional anthropology in 33 different countries, including Asia and Central America. He has taught courses in botanical medicine, nutrition and anthropology at colleges in the U.S. and Canada. Dr. Heinerman is Director of the Anthropological Research Center in Salt Lake City, Utah.

The Health Benefits of Cayenne

The amazing spice and its curative powers in colds, circulatory and digestive problems, respiratory ills, infections and more

John Heinerman, Ph.D.
Author of *The Healing Benefits of Garlic*

Keats Publishing, Inc. New Canaan, Connecticut

THE HEALTH BENEFITS OF CAYENNE

Copyright © 1997 by John Heinerman, Ph.D.

ISBN: 0-87983-703-9

Keats Good Health Guides are published by
Keats Publishing, Inc.
27 Pine Street (Box 876)
New Canaan, Connecticut 06840-0876
Keats Publishing website address: www.keats.com

17 18 19 20 21 22 QVS/QVS 21 20 19 18 17

Contents

In the quarter-century or more that I've been dealing with botanicals on a fairly regular basis, I've always looked upon cayenne pepper as something of an enigma. Where else would you find something so intensely hot that it makes your lips, mouth and throat seem on fire? But at the same it is able to manifest a *refrigerant* action on the body in very warm and humid climates to the point of actually *cooling* a person down somewhat. Sound impossible? Not at all, because I've tested this remedy for myself many times while trekking around in jungles of Central America on various expeditions in search of new botanicals and more folk remedies.

It was an old Maya *curandero* or native healer in the highlands of Guatemala in 1977 who first showed me how to use cayenne in some food or beverage for this purpose. I'll have to admit it was plenty hot going down, but a few hours later I noticed that my physical system was better able to cope with the intense heat and stifling humidity than it had been before.

This is an herb with apparently contradictory action. Consider this: cayenne is able to promote better circulation internally, but can also halt hemorrhaging just as well by expediting the clotting process. I've seen equally amazing but opposite results. An elderly gentleman suffering from coldness in his extremities starts taking two capsules of cayenne pepper every morning with his breakfast and soon feels warmth in those regions as circulation increases. An eleven-year-old boy accidentally shoots himself with his father's service revolver. The frantic mother quickly dumps at least a cup of cayenne into the wound and feels a measure of reassurance come over her when the bleeding slows down long enough for him to be rushed to the nearest hospital by ambulance.

In mythology, Janus was an ancient Roman god of gates and beginnings, represented with two opposite faces, one scowling and one smiling. In some ways cayenne has similar attributes that seem to oppose each other. If a small amount is moistened with some water and then applied topically to the surface of the skin, it will produce localized inflammation and certain discomfort. On the other hand, the very same factor (capsaicin) that gives this spice its rubefacient quality also brings countless relief to millions of rheumatoid arthritis sufferers by helping to reduce painful joint swelling and inflammation. In fact, capsaicin is the key ingredient in many new topical applications intended solely for arthritic relief.

Capsaicinoids are the naturally occurring compounds that give cayenne pepper its pungency and chiles the thermonuclear capability of nearly blowing your lips half way across the room (if you're not used to them). Having virtually no odor or flavor, they act directly on pain receptors located in the mouth and throat. Research has shown that nordihydrocapsaicin (NDHC) is the mildest and "least provoking." It is also only about 50 percent as hot as capsaicin and dihydrocapsaicin (DHC); the latter two are the most intense and prevalent capsaicinoids.

NDHC has been described as "mellow warming" from the moment it is swallowed; the effect recedes pretty quickly and then becomes more localized towards the front of the mouth and palate. Generally speaking, the character of this weak capsaicinoid is "fruity, sweet and spicy," claim cayenne and chile lovers. In contrast, another capsaicinoid, homodihydrocapsaicin (HDHC) is slightly more subtle: it almost creeps in unawares "on little cat's feet" and doesn't immediately deliver its potent sting. When it does, however, a few moments later, the strong numbing, burning sensation can be felt in the throat and back of the tongue and palate. HDHC's pungency is also the most prolonged and difficult to rinse out.

But the two hottest little numbers in cayenne pepper and "hand grenade" chiles (as I call them, because they explode in your mouth) are by far capsaicin and DHC. Their fire spreads everywhere from the midtongue and palate back down into the throat, and is felt almost immediately.

And just how hot might that be, some may ask? Well, consider this for a moment: a *single* drop of capsaicin diluted in 100,000 drops of water will produce a persistent burning of the tongue. Diluted in a million drops of water, it still manages to produce discernible warmth. Like DHC, capsaicin's intense sting develops very quickly and lasts much longer than that of NDHC.[1]

There has always existed a little confusion between cayenne

pepper and chile peppers. Chiles all belong to the genus *Capsicum*. Capsicums include cayenne (red pepper), jalapeño, serranos, habañeros, scotch bonnets and also the mild paprika, bell peppers and virtually all other peppers you can name except black pepper. Capsicums are members of the nightshade family along with potatoes, tomatoes and eggplant. All chiles contain varying amounts of the previously referred to capsaicinoids, with capsaicin and DHC leading the pack so far as heat intensity goes. Cayenne pepper *per se (Capsicum annuum)* is just *one* of many varieties of chiles. And while most other chiles are used in their *whole* fresh or dried forms, cayenne pepper, for the most part, is nearly always used in *powdered* form for culinary and medicinal purposes.

A good rule of thumb to remember is this: the *smaller* the chile, the hotter it's going to be. That's due to the fact that smaller chiles have a larger amount of seeds and vein (or internal rib) relative to larger chiles, and these are the parts that contain up to 80 percent of the capsaicin. Let's start with a big chile, say the Hungarian sweet kind, which measures about six inches in length; on the heat scale it registers 0 to 1. Now let's move on *down* to cayenne pepper, which averages about three inches in length: its rating on the heat scale quickly picks up to a peppery 8. Finally, we come to the itty-bitty lantern-shaped habañero, which averages about 1½ inches in length; fire alarms sound all through the body because of the perfect 10 heat intensity that it packs. In fact, a habañero is 30 to 50 times hotter than the hottest jalapeño on record![2]

HISTORICAL BACKGROUND

Great discoveries have often occurred during individual quests for knowledge. Consider what we learned about the moon from the Apollo 13 landing and takeoff. European taste buds were treated to more lively foods when the fabled Venetian, Marco Polo, began a twenty-year journey to the Orient in 1271. This journey would eventually open the doors to new sources of exotic spices, thereby bypassing the exclusive control which the Arabs had had on that rich trade for many centuries.

The trip of Cristobal Colón (anglicized to Christopher Columbus) to the New World introduced wealthy Europeans to a pair of new aromatic plants that enriched their repertory of seasonings considerably. Those plants were peppers and allspice, both of which the Europeans called pimiento. But, oddly enough, only peppers were considered at that time to be of any practical worth. A later trip by Colón added the vanilla-producing orchid, *Vanilla planifolia* to the list.

When Colón gave a full report of his first trip to the court of Ferdinand and Isabella, there was also present an Italian cleric and historian by the name of Pietro Martire D'Anghiera. Although he never actually visited the New World himself, he gathered sufficient data about it from those who had been there (including Colón) to include in his chronicle, *De orbo novo*, which wasn't published until 1511. From his account the following can be learned about the use of cayenne pepper by some New World natives:

> "Something may be said about the pepper gathered in the islands and on the continent—but it is not pepper, though it has the same strength and the flavor, and is just as much esteemed. The natives call it *axi*, it grows taller than a poppy—When it is used there is no need of Caucasian pepper. The sweet pepper is called *Boniatum*, and the hot pepper is called *Caribe*, meaning sharp and strong; for the same reasons the cannibals are called *Caribs* because they are strong."[3]

The pungent varieties of chiles and cayennes are still referred to as *aji* (the Spanish rendering of *axi*) throughout the Caribbean and much of South America even to this day.

The Spanish explorers carelessly designated this new botanical discovery pimiento after their word for black pepper, *pimienta*. To add to the confusion even more, it wasn't long before allspice was likewise called pimiento. It wasn't until several centuries later that learned men of science and botany were able to sort out this jumble of misapplied names.

Even more fascinating is the fact that when Hernando Cortez and his men invaded the Aztec capital at Mexico City, they heard the *aji* being called *chiltli*, a term used originally in the Nahuatl (Aztec) tongue. The stem CHIL refers to the *chilli* plant and also means "red hot." The TLI (the T being silent) is a suffix without significance denoting closure, as was the custom in the Nahuatl language. A Spanish botanist by the name of Francisco Hernández was the first one to use this Aztec term *chilli* in print in an official way sometime in the year 1615. Our own present word *chile* was therefore derived from this Aztec name for *aji*.

By 1500, cayenne and its related family of peppers were

being extensively cultivated in Spain and Portugal. Portuguese trading ships carried them to the Malabar coast of India; later on, Persian, Arab, Hindu and other traders brought them to Indonesia. From there, still other trading ships advanced the spread of these fiery peppers northward to Macao, China and westward to the Moluccas Islands. The Portuguese were also responsible for the introduction of the capsicums into western Africa and the Congo River Basin. According to one author: "So enthusiastically was this blistering spice received in those hot lands that its New World origin was completely forgotten and it was long regarded as native to tropical Africa and India." But, "early English colonists brought peppers with them to their new American possessions, thereby reintroducing them to the North American continent."[4]

So what Cristobal Colón took back with him to show the King and Queen of Spain, eventually came full circle 150 or so years later in the Virginia and New England colonies.

NATIVE AMERICAN AND CHINESE THERAPEUTIC USES

Cayenne pepper's common name comes from the city of Cayenne, located on Cayenne Island at the mouth of the Cayenne River. It is currently the capital of French Guiana. The natural harbor made it a bustling port of trade in timber, rum, gold, and, of course, the pepper that shares its name. At various times the city has been occupied by the French, the Portuguese and the British, all of whom did brisk business in this particular pepper.

Both the ancient and modern inhabitants of the Americas and China used cayenne therapeutically. Some uses were appropriate for the times and are of historical value only today. But other applications bear closer scrutiny because of their timeless worth in treating common health problems.

The ancient Aztecs, who inhabited the Valley of Mexico for many centuries prior to the arrival of the Spaniards, utilized cayenne pepper in a number of different ways. Public intoxication was considered to be "a crime of serious nature" and dealt with severely. In order to escape notice and avoid punishment, guilty parties (usually men) would boil up a concoction of water, corn, and (unspecified) pinches of cayenne pepper, and drink this brew when relatively cool. Within a very short time, they would quickly come out of their alcoholic stupor and be quite sober thereafter.

Jesuit scholars, who accompanied the conquistadores on

their conquests of the Americas, faithfully recorded the folk uses of numerous botanicals employed by the Aztecs and others. One of these was Fray Bernardino de Sahagún, who knew the Aztec language and compiled a voluminous work on nearly every aspect of that culture that he observed within his lifetime. In Book 6 (on "Rhetoric and Moral Philosophy") of his *General History of the Things of New Spain*, Sahagún related a great deal about Aztec parenting.

He reported that one technique frequently used to punish a misbehaving child was to put a pinch of cayenne pepper on the youngster's tongue and instruct him or her to hold it in the mouth until told by an adult to swallow it. The Catholic friar noted that seldom was there a recurrence of the same misbehavior following this treatment. He also observed that if an older youth spoke arrogantly to an adult, his or her lips would be rubbed hard with plenty of cayenne pepper to remind the offender that the misspoken words stung the hearer as much as the pepper did the young person's lips. And if an offense was serious enough to warrant a whipping, cayenne pepper would sometimes be rubbed into the lacerations to intensify the punishment.[5] In today's society, however, such adult responses to youthful problems like these would be met with fierce resistance and considered flagrant child abuse.

Cayenne also occupied a strange role in punishing crimes such as treason, rebellion, homicide, adultery and homosexuality, all of which were punishable by death. If the criminal were a nobleman of some high stature in Aztec society, he would be given a strong drink mixed with adequate cayenne pepper. This fermented and fiery *pulque* would work as an anesthesia prior to scheduled execution and help to minimize pain and suffering. Common criminals, though, were offered no such relief and had to endure the full agonies of their deaths.

In the late 1970s, I did field research as a medical anthropologist among the Maya Indians of the Yucatan and the Guatemalan Highlands. I was accompanied by a medical anthropologist from Spain who spoke fluent Spanish, Mayan and English; his name was Dr. Francisco Marcos Navarette, on sabbatical leave from the University of Madrid. In one Yucatan village, we were told of an effective antidote for reversing the immediate blindness induced by eye contact with the sap of the poisonwood tree. A tiny amount of cayenne pepper was placed under each eyelid and kept there for a number of hours until vision was fully restored. Admittedly, it was an excruciatingly painful treatment, but the alternative—permanent loss of eyesight—seemed worse, therefore, justifying such use of cayenne.

The Guatemalan Maya used the leaves of the capsicum plant as a remedy for heatstroke and inflammation. Both the leaves and the pepper fruit of capsicum were applied externally for boils, abscesses, and open sores. The leaves and/or the pepper itself were frequently put on an infected cut or wound to promote quicker healing. Cayenne pepper was used to settle upset stomach and applied topically to treat lower back pain. The Maya also had their own "queer ways" of disciplining unruly children: They would rub red pepper on a disobedient child's bare skin, causing a sensation of intense burning.

There were many intriguing uses for cayenne pepper by a number of South American Indian tribes, most of whom have since become extinct in the last half-century or more. The tribes inhabited much of the huge Amazon River Basin and lived virtually undisturbed until greedy opportunists began invading their homelands in search of precious gold and valuable hardwoods.

The natives subsisted primarily on caiman (South American crocodiles, whose tails were especially relished), turtles, lizards, boa constrictors, deer, monkeys, jaguars, birds, fish, maize, bananas and nuts. The only condiments for flavoring such foods were a wild species of cayenne pepper and salt. The caiman tails, monkey brains, snake meat and lizard guts were subjected to more than the usual amounts of cayenne pepper to improve their taste.

Cayenne pepper was routinely used at one time by *Mascushi* shamans as a stimulant for getting rid of headaches; they crushed pepper fruit, soaked it in some water and then poured the mixture into the nostrils. The *Piro* combined a little water and some cayenne pepper with the brains in monkey skulls and drank this odd mixture to keep from getting sick. The *Yameo* made "a sauce of red pepper, grubs, and maize flour" with which to flavor most of their foods.

Other tropical forest tribes elsewhere in the Amazon had their own uses for cayenne pepper. The *Tupi* along the Brazilian coast at one time used a "long pepper which is crushed together with salt, pinches of which are swallowed after each mouthful" of food to prevent any indigestion from occurring afterwards. The *Trumai* and the *Nambicuara* ate cayenne pepper fruit (whole) to ward off dysentery and malaria. The *Paressi* Indians mixed cayenne pepper with their curare to make an efficient arrow or dart poison by which to bring down wild game or birds. Witch doctors of the *Chocó* tribe sometimes discreetly administered pakurú-neará, a cardiac poison, to their enemies and then cordially invited them to sit down to a meal heavily flavored with cayenne pepper so that the plant toxin would work faster. The enhanced blood circulation by cayenne helped deliver the poison more readily. The *Cawahib* sprinkled cayenne pepper on those parts of their bodies where leeches or ticks had become attached in order to have them drop off or back out more quickly.

Current tribes of the Northwest Amazon still rely on capsicum for different health or social needs:

The Mayna Jivaros of Peru apply the pepper fruit directly to the teeth to treat toothaches.

Andokes' shamans mix cayenne pepper with dried stinging nettle to hasten difficult childbirth.

The Waorani use capsicum to help overcome the after effects of intoxication with the hallucinogenic drink prepared from a plant called Banisteriopsis.

The Taiwanos grind the pepper fruit and put the powder in foods to relieve "right side" abdominal pain (appendicitis, perhaps).

The natives of the Rio Apaporis eat cayenne pepper raw to relieve flatulence and to breathe easier.[6]

In the dark and mystical world of Amazonian shamanism, cayenne pepper has always occupied a unique position. Native beliefs throughout this gigantic rain forest region hold that the capsicums animate the spirit within man by invigorating his body. Through such reanimation, the natives believe, there can come a heightened spiritual awareness of the surrounding invisible world. The capsicums have been routinely mixed with any number of different plant hallucinogens to induce a "vision quest" by which a shaman or other person can communicate more easily with unseen beings. As one shaman so eloquently put it, "it [cayenne pepper] makes my spirituality so much easier and less laborious." The topic has been dealt with elsewhere at greater length.[7]

On the other side of the world, in China, we learn that cayenne pepper was introduced several centuries ago. It was then called *fan jiao* or "barbarian's spice." The name was later changed to another colloquial term, *la qie*, which signifies "pungent eggplant," because of its similarity in shape to an eggplant. Currently, cayenne is known as *la jiao* or "pungent spice," which aptly describes its hot characteristic.[5]

You can see how the Chinese utilize cayenne pepper for food flavoring if you live in any large city such as New York, Chicago, Los Angeles, or San Francisco—all of which have their own Chinatowns. In restaurants you're apt to find a variety of pork and beef dishes on the menus which are famous for their spiciness. This spiciness comes from the liberal use of cayenne pepper by the skilled chefs who make up these dishes in just a matter of minutes. The Szechwan style of cooking is always more spicy than is the Cantonese.

I happen to prefer such food and frequently dine out at Chinese restaurants. I've noticed that certain of the hot dishes flavored with cayenne pepper have medicinal benefits beyond satisfying my appetite and giving me strength. During a bout with the flu, I eat curry chicken to abate any low-grade fever that might be present in my body. And any of the kung pao dishes (shrimp, fish, pork, or chicken) will certainly clear up lung congestion within just a few hours. If I'm still feeling weak from my cold or flu, I may have some Mongolian beef, which not only provides badly needed nourishment but also gets my bowels working regularly within a very short time. In fact, just about any of the Szechwan dishes will soon correct the worst case of constipation.

This is a clear-cut case of food therapy—letting your food become your best medicine. I've discovered that some of the best remedies for gastrointestinal problems due to infections or parasites are those cuisines which are spiked with plenty of cayenne pepper. Japanese, Korean, Thai, Vietnamese and Indonesian foods are known for their hot dishes; so, too, is Mexican food and what has been referred to as Tex-Mex cooking. The latter is a combination of Texan and Mexican styles that rely heavily on cayenne and chile peppers and is very popular throughout the American Southwest. Such items, in their time and place, when consumed moderately, can be helpful in reducing the risks of stroke, angina and thrombosis; eliminating worms from the intestinal tract, healing stomach ulcers, improving blood circulation and promoting healthier waste elimination from the body.

A visit to a Chinese herb shop or a practitioner of the Oriental healing arts will reveal a surprising number of remedies in which cayenne pepper is readily employed. Toronto-based Dr. Li Yu makes a useful preparation for treating bruises, bumps and sprains. He adds one teaspoon of powdered cayenne pepper to five tablespoons of melted Vaseline. When it congeals, he instructs his patients to apply it twice daily over the injured site until improvement is noticed. The same liniment is sometimes applied externally to treat mumps in children and leg ulcers in older people with poor circulation.

David Tao, a Chinese herbalist from Vancouver, British Columbia, recommends that those afflicted with severe mucus accumulation in their lungs try adding a pinch of cayenne pepper to one cup of hot black tea; he claims it helps to dispel the phlegm very quickly. For those suffering from the effects of frostbite on their ears, nose, fingers and toes he suggests another remedy: To one quart of boiling water, add one-half teaspoon of cayenne and simmer on low heat for five minutes; strain and wash the afflicted body parts while still warm, using cotton balls or a clean cloth to do so.

A Chinese doctor, in Albuquerque, New Mexico, recommends a very simple but effective snakebite remedy he has had occasion to use every so often. "I tell anyone who has been bitten by something as bad as a rattlesnake," he stated, "to just mix a little powdered cayenne with some of their own saliva and then apply this directly over the punctured skin where the fang marks are still evident. I tell the person to just rest awhile and drink plenty of fluids." He said that the mixture of saliva enzymes and pepper capsaicin renders most of the poison inert. The secret, of course, to making this work really well is "not to get excited when bitten." This is easier said than done for those who have a severe snake phobia.

Two parts of the world have been briefly looked at with regard to folk medicine applications for cayenne pepper. In both cultures (Middle and South American Indians and Oriental), such uses have arisen out of necessity through time-tested methods that have proven to be effective. While they have obvious historical merit, some of them also have important therapeutic value as well.

USES OF CAYENNE PEPPER FOR VARIOUS HEALTH CONDITIONS

As has been already shown, cayenne pepper is, indeed, a most useful therapeutic agent in the Indian cultures of Central and South America and the Oriental cultures of Southeast Asia. But such examples are only a few of the therapeutic uses of cayenne; in fact, there is a whole list of health problems for which this spice has been used in times past and proven to be very effective.

Many of these uses have their origins in the medical folklore of different societies around the world which rely on cayenne pepper and other useful herbs to effect simple healing solutions for ofttimes complex and baffling health problems. These applications fall under the scientific disciplines of medical anthropology and ethnobotany—sciences which examine how various cultures utilize plants for food and medicine.

Some of these folk medicine applications have been tested in clinical settings or else specific components of capsicum, such as capsaicin, have been carefully evaluated by doctors in human subjects. In both instances, the therapeutic efficacy of cayenne has been medically validated.

The following list of beneficial uses for this important spice should not be interpreted to represent the sole source of treatment for the problems mentioned. Nothing can ever replace competent medical care in serious conditions. But cayenne pepper does occupy a vital role in a comprehensive health care program that includes the best from conventional as well as complementary medicine.

Allergies

Scientists researching the medicinal possibilities of capsaicin (the fiery ingredient in cayenne pepper and chiles) have discovered a new use for it in nasal sprays. In such products, it reduces or even cures severe chronic allergic and nonallergic conditions that make people's noses run constantly and cause them to sneeze quite frequently. The physiological mechanisms behind such actions, however, aren't as yet clearly understood. Nasal sprays are not recommended for home use because capsaicin is so irritating. The scientists administered the spray after local anesthesia.

Angina

A number of years ago, one of the sons of the late Utah herbalist John R. Christopher shared with me an interesting use for capsicum. He was then 43 years of age and routinely suffered from angina or heart pains, which he claimed could be quite excruciating at times. He took a special cayenne tincture developed by his famous herbalist dad and within 45 minutes the pain would always cease.

His formula for making this cayenne tincture was as follows:

1. Put one ounce of dried capsicum in a glass jar.
2. Add one pint of alcohol such as 80-proof vodka.
3. Close the jar tightly and shake it four times daily.
4. Keep mixture in jar for only two weeks and no longer.

5. Strain liquid through double-layered cheesecloth.
6. Commence tincture at start of full moon for greater potency.
7. Store in amber glass bottles. Seal tightly.
8. To use, place six drops of cayenne pepper under tongue twice daily or else dilute same amount in six ounces of water or juice. Take on an empty stomach or between meals.

Note: If you are taking nitroglycerin for angina, do not discontinue medication or use this remedy without your physician's permission.

Arthritis

Animal experiments have shown that capsaicin dramatically "reduces the increase of paw diameter in rats with adjuvant arthritis." This "anti-inflammatory effect occurred within 24 hours . . . [and] persisted well over 20 days." The anti-inflammatory action was attributed to the effect of capsaicin on substance P.[8] Substance P is a nervous system-derived chemical (a peptide), released in the spinal cord as well as from the peripheral nerve endings. This neuropeptide has multiple proinflammatory properties and is released in greater quantities from pain transmission nerves (the sensory afferent nerve fiber terminals) located in knee and ankle joints, where a great deal of arthritic swelling usually occurs.[9]

Excess substance P isn't good because it breaks down the cartilage cushions in joints, contributing to osteoarthritis. It also serves as a pain neurotransmitter in both osteoarthritis and rheumatoid arthritis. In other words, overproduction of substance P in your system means you'll be feeling a great deal of pain.

However, medical researchers have discovered that capsaicin—known to chemists as trans-8-methyl-N-vanillyl-6-nonenamide—inhibits the activity of substance P.[10] Different commercial brands of cream containing various amounts of capsaicin, when rubbed on the skin, penetrate to arthritic joints where they stop the destruction of cartilage, relieve pain and increase joint flexibility.

To assess the value of such capsaicin creams, Roy Altman, M.D., of the University of Miami (Florida) School of Medicine, conducted a double-blind study on 96 arthritic patients. The patients applied either a 0.025 percent capsaicin cream or a plain cream to their arthritic joints. In the majority of cases this happened to be the knees. Most of the applications were made in a rotary massage motion four times a day.

The doctor tracked the patients' responses through precise measurements of physical movement and pain as well as through the volunteers' subjective reports (kept by themselves) about whether they felt better or worse. Patients who used the capsaicin cream had a definite reduction in pain after just two months and by the end of the study, four weeks later, over 80 percent of those applying such cream had significantly fewer arthritic symptoms including less joint stiffness in the morning. By contrast, less than 55 percent of patients using the plain cream felt better.

Asthma

A medical researcher at UCLA School of Medicine theorized that asthma, like arthritis, might be caused by an overproduction of substance P and that excess receptors for it were in the lungs.[11] Consequently, a cayenne pepper tincture similar to the one given for angina might help to relieve the belabored breathing common to asthma.

Atherosclerosis

The late Dr. John Ray Christopher, a nationally known herbalist from Utah, helped thousands of people in his lifetime regain their health through the natural means of herbs. But it was another great herbalist by the name of Dr. H. Nowell, from the Dominican Herbal College in Vancouver, British Columbia, Canada, who prescribed cayenne for Christopher's heart condition.

Ray (as his friends always called him) stated in an interview one time: "When I was 35, the doctors said I would be dead by 43. I had advanced hardening of the arteries. The veins would stick out of my hands like pencils. I also suffered from crippling arthritis, stomach ulcers and was the victim of two horrible auto accidents. No insurance company would touch me—not even for a $1,000 policy!"

Ray was then studying herbal medicine under Dr. Nowell in Vancouver, B.C. His professor showed Ray just how beneficial capsicum could be for improving human health. "I worked up to a teaspoon three times a day mixed with water," Ray would later recall. "I continued from the time I was 35 and am still using it. It was amazing! By the time I was 45 years of age, ten years after I had started using cayenne, a group wanted me to have a $100,000 policy to insure them on the business deal we were working out.

"I went for the examination. Since this was a large policy, the insurance company required two medical doctors, each to give two physicals at various times. That was a total of four physicals. I took the examination and one medical doctor, when he got through, said, 'Well, this is astounding. I see your age is 45, but you have the venous structure of a teenage boy. I've never seen anything like it!" Needless to say, Ray passed all four physicals with flying colors. Cayenne pepper had, indeed, cured him of his atherosclerosis, arthritis and ulcers for good.[12]

Dr. Christopher met an untimely death at the age of 73 from the consequences of a severe head injury incurred when he slipped on ice several years earlier.

Blood Clots

Thailand (formerly the Kingdom of Siam) is the country in Southeast Asia on which Richard Rogers and Oscar Hammerstein II based their famous Broadway musical, *The King and I*. The scene which featured a feast for the royal family correctly included some cayenne pepper. Capsicum is the most popular seasoning of Thai food and is considered by most Thai people a necessary appetizer for their everyday meals. Medical investigators have noticed a definite correlation between high capsicum consumption and extremely low thromboembolic phenomena.[13] Cayenne protects against blood clot formation by causing an increase in fibrinolytic (clot-dissolving) activity of red blood cells.

Bowel Diseases

The neurotransmitter called substance P is released from the peripheral neurons (those outside the brain and spinal cord) which transmit pain signals to the brain; this, in turn, helps regulate the response of the immune system to damaged tissue. Medical researchers from UCLA School of Medicine, the Veterans Administration Wadsworth Medical Center (both in Los Angeles) and Harvard Medical School in Boston found that people with chronic inflammatory bowel diseases have high numbers of receptors for substance P in their intestinal tissue.

With too many substance P receptors in the intestinal tract, the immune systems of such persons are apt to overreact, inducing enough inflammation to trigger the sensory neurons to send more pain signals and release more substance P. This vicious cycle eventually leads to autoimmune bowel disorders like ulcerative colitis and Crohn's disease.[11]

Nerve endings that release substance P are also present in the urinary bladder; when any inflammation occurs there, greater amounts of substance P are automatically released. But the substance P content "was strongly reduced [by] 80 percent [following] pretreatment with a high dose of capsaicin" injected beneath the skin.[14] It is believed by some scientists, who are acquainted with capsaicin's properties, that it can also substantially reduce the release of substance P in those suffering from various bowel diseases.

Bruises

A journal of traditional medicine from Zhejiang, published in Chinese in 1965, reported that seven out of a dozen patients treated with an ointment of cayenne pepper recovered from painful bruises and sprains while three others showed moderate improvement; only two cases failed to respond to the therapy. The ointment was made by combining one part of cayenne pepper powder with five parts of melted Vaseline. The mixture was thoroughly blended and then allowed to cool until it congealed again. This ointment was applied topically to the injured skin or muscle tissue once a day for about a week until results were noticed.

Cancer

Some evidence exists to show that the isolated capsaicin in cayenne pepper may be mutagenic (causing abnormal changes in cells). But there is adequate scientific proof to show that this fiery component of capsicum can protect the body against some known food and beverage chemicals that can cause cancer and induce cell mutations.[15] Also, when capsaicin is taken with plant chlorophyll, its mutagenic properties are suppressed.[16]

Common Cold/Influenza

One physician routinely prescribed cayenne pepper to many of his adult patients to prevent frequent bouts of the common cold or influenza. His prescription was very simple: At the onset of symptoms, take one teaspoon of cayenne powder in a glass of warm water with the juice of one lemon and a teaspoon of honey; stir thoroughly and drink slowly. The physician who prescribed this remedy said it never failed to prevent the development of colds and flus in those who faithfully adhered to this practical recommendation.[17]

Also, the renowned grandma's chicken soup, when laced with adequate capsicum, garlic, and onion, is known to help cure even the most stubborn cold or flu. Chicken soup has been tested clinically and proven to work. But not just any old chicken soup will do. The spicier it is, the better for you. The cayenne helps to flush out the bacteria and viruses responsible for the cold or flu by causing eyes to water, skin to sweat, nose to run, and lungs to discharge. This rush of fluids from the body carries out the invisible microbes responsible for such infections.[18]

Congestive Heart Failure

On May 30, 1978, at the age of 42, Richard F. Quinn suffered a near-fatal heart attack. An angiogram revealed a 98 percent blockage of the main artery leading to his heart. He underwent emergency bypass surgery. After that, he "ate no fat, thought no bad thoughts, avoided stress, exertion and excitement . . . and went for slow walks." But, in spite of all this, he got progressively weaker.

Then, in October 1978, Quinn suffered symptoms typical of congestive heart failure—fainting, dizziness, and temporary blindness that lasted from 30 minutes to an hour or more. Frightened out of his wits, he promptly consulted with a cardiologist, who correctly diagnosed his problem but could offer little advice as to how to treat it except with prescribed medication, which was refused by his patient.

Quinn did some research on his own and learned how cayenne pepper had helped others in similar situations. He purchased some from a local health food store and started taking three capsules of capsicum daily with meals. That was back in 1978; some 18 years later, his heart was still "as good as new," and he said he felt "like a kid all over again, with energy and stamina I never before believed possible for a recovering heart patient to have."[30]

Diabetes

Certain medicinal herbs are known for their strong hypoglycemic actions: garlic and onion, goldenseal and pau d'arco. Another equally potent hypoglycemic agent is cayenne pepper. When powdered extracts of this important spice were given to mongrel street dogs "a significant hypoglycaemic effect" was exhibited in all animals within 30 minutes or less.[19] For those suffering from diabetes mellitus, this comes as welcome news. A recommended dose of cayenne for diabetic sufferers is two to four capsules daily with meals. The "hypoglycemic effect" means the cayenne *lowered blood sugar* which is what insulin does because diabetics have *high blood sugar*. But for those already suffering from low blood sugar, cayenne is best avoided!

Diabetic Neuropathy

Recent medical findings suggest that the topical application of capsaicin cream is quite safe and very effective in the treatment of pain ordinarily observed in patients experiencing diabetic neuropathy.[20,21] In one of these recent studies involving almost a thousand patients attending a diabetic clinic, a full 25 percent reported having chronic pain, but nearly a quarter of these had never received any treatment for their pain. While several therapies have been used to treat the pain often associated with diabetic neuropathy, most have been of limited success in relieving discomfort and have intolerable side effects, especially in the aged. Double-blind, controlled trials with relatively large numbers of patients at a number of medical centers around the country have demonstrated a very beneficial effect of capsaicin cream in relieving those pains associated with diabetic polyneuropathy.[22]

Duodenal Ulcers

Lee Klatt, age 59, of Twin Rivers, Wisconsin, put up with his duodenal ulcers for two decades. But then he learned about cayenne pepper from a radio disc jockey, who enjoyed promoting the virtues of capsicum over the airwaves. Klatt began taking four capsules three times daily with meals and leveled off to half this amount in four months. Not only did his ulcers disappear but his blood circulation improved dramatically. A 1991 study conducted by Kyoto Pharmaceutical University in Japan demonstrated that when capsaicin was given regularly, it increased the flow of protective mucus within the gut, thereby helping to heal duodenal ulcers.[23]

Elevated Cholesterol

The American diet contains a higher fat content than that considered safe by most doctors. The cholesterol-reducing properties of capsaicin have been studied by Indian biochemists and reported in the scientific literature.[24]

Groups of lab rats were fed natural or synthetic capsaicin in diets with a fat content ranging from 10 to 30 percent. The natural capsaicin (8-methyl, N-vanillyl, 6-none-namide) and synthetic (N-vanillyl nonanamide) prevented any significant rise in liver cholesterol. Both forms were also responsible for causing elevated fecal excretions of free cholesterol and bile acids from the liver and gall bladder.

The scientists studying this remarkable lipid-lowering action concluded that capsaicin may, indeed, "prove to be of value in human dietary [needs]" and in the prevention of cholesterol-associated heart diseases such as arteriosclerosis and its more advanced form of atherosclerosis. It is worth noting here, that capsaicin shares a similar chemical component (a vanillyl moiety) with gingerol (from ginger root) and curcumin (an antioxidant from turmeric), both of which also reduce serum cholesterol levels.

Elevated Triglycerides

Much attention has been given the negative impact of excess cholesterol on the heart by the news media. Cholesterol, especially the LDL or so called "bad" cholesterol, can seriously injure heart arteries over many years. Medical researchers are also looking at the role of triglycerides in coronary artery disease and finding that these, more than cholesterol itself, may be to blame. (Triglycerides are neutral fats synthesized from carbohydrates for storage in body fat cells. When broken up by enzymatic action, they release free fatty acids in the blood.)

A similar experiment with rodents fed a diet containing 30 percent pure lard showed drastic reductions in animal serum triglycerides when they were simultaneously given capsaicin.[25]

Fatigue

General and chronic fatigue afflicts about 35 percent of the American population on a consistent basis. Such a problem is often viral-induced (herpes), caused by a fungal (*Candida albicans*) infection, lack of adequate sleep or low blood sugar (hypoglycemia). More often than not, the factors behind continual fatigue are multiple in scope.

Capsaicin, by itself, can be very hypoglycemic (see information given under DIABETES). But when used in combination with *equal* amounts of ginseng and gotu kola, capsaicin can increase biochemical endurance during periods of emotional and physical stress. Animal and human models on whom this unique blend of herbs has been tested displayed virtually *no* fatigue during exercises that were intended to be very stressful and energy-draining.

Free Radical Activity

Free radicals may be considered as invisible molecular sharks zipping about in our cellular seas, creating havoc and destruction wherever they go. But a group of compounds known as antioxidants effectively check the free-roaming and ravaging behavior of free radicals. Capsorubin, a carotenoid associated with capsaicin in cayenne pepper, functions as an excellent antioxidant that diminishes the potentially harmful actions of these misguided molecules.[26]

Frostbite/Frozen Limbs

In the early days of frontier America, it was quite common for people to sustain freezing of their lower extremities when traveling during periods of cold weather and snow. Gangrene would then quickly set in, necessitating the prompt amputation of frozen limbs in order to save human life. But in one particular case, one pioneer doctor, Priddy Meeks, felt inspired to use cayenne pepper with his patient, which not only saved the man's life but also his damaged feet. His story was related in the *Utah Historical Quarterly*.

"James McCann, a young man, came to me with both feet frozen above his ankles. It was thought there was no possible chance to save his life without amputation of both feet. I was at my wits end to know what to do. I saw no possible chance for avoiding amputation. On impulse I decided to give him cayenne pepper inwardly and see what effect that would have on the frozen feet.

"I commenced by giving him rather small doses at first, about three times a day. It increased the warmth and power of action in the blood to such a degree that it gave him such pain and misery in his legs that he could not bear it. He lay down on his back and elevated his feet up against the wall for three or four days and then he could sit up in a chair. The frozen flesh would rot and rope down from his foot when it would be on his knee, clear down to the floor, just like a buckwheat batter, and the new flesh would form as fast as the dead flesh would get out of the way. In fact the new flesh would seem to crowd the dead flesh out of the way to make room for the new flesh.

"That was all the medical treatment he had and to my astonishment and to every one else that knew of the circumstances, the sixteenth day after I gave him the first dose of pepper he walked nine miles and said that he could have walked as far again. He lost but five toenails all told. Now the healing power of nature is in the blood and to accelerate the blood is to accelerate the healing power of nature and I am convinced that there is nothing that will do this like cayenne pepper; you will find it applicable in all cases of sickness."

Headaches
Italian researchers at the University of Florence employed nasal sprays containing tiny amounts of capsaicin to treat the intense pain of cluster headaches, which can be frequent and lengthy. The excruciating pain concentrates on one side of the head, typically around an eye. In the Italian study, the spray was squirted into the nostril on the affected side of the head of twenty-nine cluster headache patients. Thirteen subjects received the spray in the nostril opposite the side of the head that felt the pain, and they experienced no improvement in their situation. In eleven patients treated on the affected side, the headaches ceased altogether and in two more the headache frequency was reduced by at least 50 percent.[27]

In a different study, patients who had capsaicin ointment applied to their temples were headache-free during days when they normally would have had pain. The ointment raised the temperature at the temples, which ordinarily experience a heat loss during cluster attacks. Capsaicin creams that may be useful for treating headaches are marketed under trade names like Zostrix and Axsain as over-the-counter drugs. When using such products on the forehead or around the temples, it is a good idea to keep them away from the eyes to prevent stinging.[28]

Head Congestion
A useful remedy from the Maya Indians of Belize in Central America calls for a warm tea (one-half cup of hot water) made from cayenne pepper (one-eighth teaspoon) to be used in breaking up congestion in the nose, head and sinuses.

Heart Arrhythmias
Scientists working for the Bristol-Myers Squibb Pharmaceutical Research Institute in Princeton, New Jersey, administered varying amounts of capsaicin to animals suffering from various kinds of serious heart arrhythmias. It was reported that the capsaicin reduced ventricular tachycardias and ventricular fibrillations. Capsaicin also dramatically improved blood flow to the heart. Capsaicin seems to function as a natural calcium blocker, analogous to the effect of some prescription heart drugs.[29]

Heart Attack

The late Utah herbalist Dr. John R. Christopher made the following comments about cayenne pepper some years ago. "I have used cayenne so many times . . . with such success . . . in 35 years of practice [that] I have never on house calls lost one heart attack patient." His method was simple enough: (1) Steep one teaspoon of powdered cayenne in one cup of hot water until it's cool enough to drink; (2) If the patient can breathe normally, prop up the patient and pour the cayenne tea down the person's throat. Usually within a couple of minutes the heart attack will have ceased. While this measure has proven effective in the hands of skilled folk healers, it is not recommended in the hands of the unskilled. Consult a physician immediately when faced with symptoms of heart attack.[20]

Heart Disease

Epidemiologists (scientists who study disease relationships) have observed that there is considerably less incidence of heart disease in New Mexico than in other states. Thailand ranks near the bottom for the same disease statistics. In both places, there is very heavy use of cayenne pepper by the respective populations.

Heatstroke

Cayenne pepper, a familiar medicinal and culinary spice with well-known *heating* properties, can produce an opposite reaction. When taken in small amounts, it stimulates circulation and the digestive processes. But, when consumed in large amounts it will cause a cooling effect. This helps to explain why people living in hot tropical climates are apt to eat a lot of this particular spice.

The cooling sensation is produced in two different ways. In one way the body (especially the face) starts to sweat; the more perspiration that gathers on the skin, the cooler a person will feel. The other way is through the release of endorphins by capsaicin into the bloodstream of people who eat cayenne pepper. These natural opiates in the brain affect the body's own internal temperature, lowering it a few degrees.

Hemorrhaging

The late Utah herbalist Dr. John R. Christopher was a strong proponent of cayenne pepper, believing it to stop bleeding better than anything else in the plant kingdom with which he was familiar. He told the story of an eight-year-old boy who had been accidentally shot while playing a game of "Cops and Robbers" with his father's handgun. His sister had the good sense to mix a tablespoon of cayenne with a glass of water and forced her brother to drink it. He was rushed by ambulance to a big city hospital some 18 miles distant, where he underwent immediate surgery to repair the damage which the bullet had caused to his abdomen. Doctors were astonished to discover that there was *no* massive internal bleeding as expected, but only a small amount of blood that had collected there before the cayenne pepper took affect.[20]

Herpes Zoster

The herpes family of viruses has been around a very, very long time on this planet. It is believed by some paleontologists, in fact, to have existed during the Jurassic Era and may have infected dinosaurs to some extent.

The varicella zoster type is responsible for two very distinct clinical disorders, namely primary varicella (otherwise known as chicken pox) and zoster (shingles). This particular kind of herpes virus is capable of affecting nerves and causing organ damage and severe pain that can last for months or even years.

Cayenne pepper capsules taken internally (two daily with food) or the topical application of any capsaicin cream (daily) will help to minimize agonizing pain that can persist during and long after the viral infection has disappeared.[30]

Hypertension

The late Dr. Christopher told compelling stories about cayenne pepper that were always enjoyable to listen to. He told of a famous black belt karate expert who suffered from a history of high blood pressure and started using capsicum on Dr. Christopher's advice. Within just four months, his blood pressure had returned completely to normal, much to the astonishment of his own doctor![20]

Indigestion

In the early-to-middle part of the 19th century there thrived an eclectic system of alternative medicine known as Thomsonian medicine. One of its outstanding features was the *limited* number of primary herbs repeatedly utilized, although many other secondary herbs were used occasionally. Samuel Thomson, the system's founder, recommended cayenne pepper and goldenseal root for their excellent healing properties.

Of cayenne he said: "I am perfectly convinced that [cayenne

pepper] is the best thing that can be used . . . to produce a natural digestion of the food which will nourish the body, establish perspiration, and restore the health of the patient. I found it to be perfectly safe in all cases, and have never known any bad effects to arise from its use." He frequently used it in cases involving disturbances of the gastrointestinal tract.

A medical study conducted in 1988 at the Baylor College of Medicine in Houston, Texas, demonstrated how cayenne might assist in the digestive processes. It was found that the capsaicin in the red pepper dramatically increased gastric secretions within the gut but did no actual harm.[31] More specifically, the number of goblet cells (mucus-secreting cells) in the duodenum portion of the gut increased in the presence of capsaicin. There was an enhanced discharge of mucus from these cells in response to this treatment.[32]

Infection

Anyone at all familiar with the role of vitamin C in the health care process knows that it is the number one nutrient for warding off or treating existing infections in the body. But what isn't so well known is the part that a species of capsicum played in its discovery.

Hungarian biochemist Albert Szent-Györgyi had been studying enzymes for years when he identified an active chemical which he labeled "hexuronic acid." He had crystallized small amounts of it from cabbages, turnips, oranges and—most successfully—from the adrenal glands of cattle. But he could never get enough for further experiments.

He gave his last teaspoon of hexuronic acid to a young Hungarian-American by the name of Joseph Lewis Svirbely, who frugally meted this out over the next couple of months to a clutch of guinea pigs threatened with scurvy (or were "scorbutic"). To his astonishment, the animals thrived. Both men quickly recognized that hexuronic acid *was* the missing nutrient and the chemical was quickly renamed ascorbic acid (vitamin C).

"There we were," Szent-Györgyi recalled later on in life. "Ascorbic acid seemed medically most important but there was none of it around." By accident, his wife helped him win a Nobel prize while his colleague sank into virtual obscurity.

"One night my wife fixed me some fresh red pepper for supper. I didn't feel like eating it, so I took it to the lab." There, on a hunch, Szent-Györgyi assayed his dinner of paprika and found that the pepper contained nearly seven times more vitamin C than adrenal glands and eight times more than lemons. Within a fortnight he had pounds of the pure vitamin, enough to send to researchers worldwide for use in analysis and manufacture. In 1996, United States consumption alone was 16,500 tons of synthetic vitamin C. It was one of the capsicums that made it all possible.[33]

Itching

People who suffer severe itches from such medical conditions as pruritus, notalgia parasthetica, and lichen simplex chronicus experience noticeable improvement when treated topically with any of the capsaicinoid creams currently on the market. These remedies appear to work partly because the capsaicinoids interfere with the nerves' ability to transmit messages to the brain. With this channel of communication temporarily impaired, the sensation of itching ceases altogether.

Lumbago

Native practitioners in some West African countries have utilized cotton or wool which has been impregnated with capsaicin to successfully treat cases of lumbago, neuralgia, or rheumatism. The treated material is applied to the skin and left on for 20 minutes.

Motion Sickness

Cayenne pepper is quite effective in dealing with motion sickness. A teaspoonful of cayenne in a tablespoon of olive oil taken internally at the first sign of nausea will help to prevent further symptoms of sea- or airsickness. Or one-half teaspoonful each of cayenne and ginger root in the same medium (or flaxseed, canola, or sunflower oil) works just as effectively.

Mouth Sores

Oral stomatitis is a very painful condition of mouth sores caused by cancer chemotherapy and radiation treatments. The sores can be overwhelming to the point that some individuals can't chew food and must, therefore, cease treatment for their cancers. But in a very innovative way, capsaicin was used to treat this serious problem in cancer patients.

Yale University medical researcher Dr. Tracy Karrer had already demonstrated that the fiery component in cayenne could eliminate such oral pain. A stock market analyst turned medical student, Wolffe Nadoolman, thought up the idea to administer capsaicin through candy. Karrer obtained the needed spice and at the metabolic kitchen at Yale's General Clinical Research Center, cooked up butterscotch brittle with capsaicin according to instructions given to him by Nadoolman. Cancer patients from the Comprehensive Cancer Center, who consumed the candy with delight, reported feeling *no* more pain afterwards![34]

Multiple Sclerosis

An alternative-minded medical doctor from Louisiana (who asked not to be identified by name) told me that he had been using cayenne pepper with some of his patients who had been diagnosed with multiple sclerosis (MS) in the *early* stages *only*. By having them take four capsules of cayenne each day with food for several months, their symptoms subsided to a remarkable degree, but didn't entirely disappear. He believed the capsaicin was in some way responsible for this, but couldn't explain how it worked.

Nerve Inflammation

Capsaicin is capable of reducing the sensation of painful inflammation in the sensory nerves and the pain-sensitive nerve terminals. Both topical creams and oral supplementation appear to work equally well to achieve this.

Neuralgia

Controlled studies have demonstrated that topically applied capsaicin is a very safe and effective treatment for neuralgia. In one double-blind experiment 32 elderly patients with chronic neuralgia were treated with either capsaicin cream or a similar appearing placebo for six weeks. Response to treatment was evaluated by visual analogue scales of pain and of pain relief, together with changes in a categoric pain scale and by a physician's global evaluation. Significantly greater relief in the capsaicin-treated group than in the placebo group was observed for all efficacy variables. After the six-week program nearly 80 percent of the capsaicin-treated patients had experienced considerable relief from their neuralgic pain.[35]

Night Blindness

This clearly is in the realm of medical hearsay, better known as folklore, but is probably worth mentioning. The half-Incan, half-Spanish historian Garcilaso de la Vega described what he had heard from someone else in 1609: "I heard a Spaniard from Mexico declare that cayenne pepper was very good for the sight, so he used to eat two roasted peppers as a sort of dessert after every meal." In my own travels throughout Mexico doing folk medicine research, I've had a number of Indians tell me that their regular consumption of cayenne and chile peppers kept their eyesight from failing as they grew older.

Obesity

Researchers at the Oxford Polytechnic in Oxford, England discovered that capsaicin can help to burn up extra calories in a way similar to what exercise does. They therefore recommended that those who are overweight or having a "battle with the bulge" consume cayenne and chile peppers fairly regularly in order to "grow thin."

Pain

For the past several years, a growing body of medical evidence has been gathering; demonstrating capsaicin's unique ability to stop the sensation of pain within the body. This finding suggests that surgeons may one day be able to slather capsaicin-like compounds on the skin of burn patients or smear them into the incisions of patients undergoing routine operations.

Researchers at Johns Hopkins University School of Medicine in Baltimore injected a capsaicin analog beneath the surface of the skin of one inner forearm of each of eight volunteers. The volunteers received a control injection of an inactive substance in the other inner forearm. They reported reduced pain sensation in the forearm treated with capsaicin following a burn on each arm equivalent to touching a hot stove. By the next day, the capsaicin-treated arm was much less sensitive to touch and heat than the control arm.

Capsaicin works by desensitizing small-diameter nerve fibers, the ones responsible for pain. But it has no effect on large-diameter nerve fibers.[36] Some capsaicin products currently being looked at include special anesthetic creams that can be rubbed on the shoulders or buttocks of young children receiving shots, or on the stump ends of amputees to help end so called "phantom limb pains."

Peptic Ulcer

New research now suggests that capsicum might actually protect against peptic ulcers, advice that obviously flies in the face of conventional wisdom. Numerous experiments have demonstrated how effectively the spice's fiery component protects the gastric mucosal membrane against damage from alcohol and aspirin. One Singapore medical researcher thinks that the constituent may accomplish this by stimulating a hormone that increases blood flow and nourishes the gastric mucosal membrane.[10] People aware of this research who suffer from this problem have found considerable relief by taking one capsule of cayenne with every meal.

Poor Appetite
Indonesian scientists discovered that by mixing tiny amounts of cayenne pepper with various foods, it made them more appetizing to those who had no real desire to eat. Those using capsicum with their meals ate more heartily than those who didn't.

Psoriasis
The prescription cream Zostrix (from GenDerm), whose active ingredient is capsaicin, has helped a number of older people suffering from psoriasis and shingles. When the cream was applied topically, it blocked the synthesis and nerve transport of substance P, the chemical largely responsible for the skin pain induced by these diseases.[37]

Respiratory Disorders
The ancient Maya of the Yucatan Peninsula and the Guatemalan Highlands routinely incorporated cayenne pepper into their materia medica for the treatment of asthma, bronchitis, coughs, colds, sore throats and other respiratory disorders without ever knowing the basis for its effectiveness. But today, scientists think that the principal component, capsaicin, acts as an irritant in the lungs to help dislodge hard-to-remove mucus deposits.[4]

Shingles
Medical investigators at the pain clinic in Toronto General Hospital in eastern Canada applied a capsaicinoid-cream to their patients' shingles-sensitive skin. Close to 80 percent of their patients reported immediate relief and another 56 percent experienced a substantial decline in their pain.

Stomach Ulcer (also see Peptic Ulcer)
Some medical experts assume that the consumption of cayenne pepper or hot chiles might aggravate the condition of

those suffering from duodenal ulcers. But doctors at an Indian hospital in New Delhi found no differences between two groups of ulcer patients involved in an experiment with cayenne pepper. Both groups were fed a normal hospital diet, but one group received a daily supplement of three grams of capsicum. Weekly comparisons were made between both groups. At the end of a month, the rate of ulcer healing was identical for both. Patients who received the cayenne displayed no gastric mucosal abnormalities or erosions. (Three grams of cayenne is a standard amount consumed in the typical Indian diet every day.)[38]

Toothache
About one-and-a-half centuries ago, the Irish developed a great remedy for instant relief from excruciating toothache. One level teaspoon of cayenne pepper was combined with one pint of strong Irish whiskey and left to sit for two weeks, being thoroughly shaken every day. The solution was then strained into another bottle and stored until needed in a cool, dark, dry place. About four drops of this pepper extract could be put on a piece of cotton and inserted into the mouth onto the infected tooth. Within minutes, the distressing pain disappeared!

For the truly brave of heart, however, there is an even quicker way to accomplish this that was borrowed from ancient times. Nero (born Lucius Domitius Ahenobarbus), one of Rome's most decadent emperors and the one ultimately responsible for the Great Fire that burned much of that city to the ground, sometimes put a generous pinch of cayenne pepper into his mouth to relieve any toothache he had. Many of this tyrant's desperate acts reflected an insanity, but this wasn't one of them.

HELPFUL HOME REMEDIES

Over the years that I have studied medicinal plants in America and many other countries, I've accumulated a collection of helpful remedies involving cayenne pepper. They are for different problems than those previously cited.

Abscesses/Boils
Apply cayenne pepper fluid extract to the abscess or boil. It will bring the stigma to a head as well as aid the drying and mending process.

Abrasions

Sprinkle a tiny amount of cayenne pepper on a small clean cut to stop the bleeding and promote healing.

Asthma Attack

A friend and colleague, Jim Duke, Ph.D., now retired from the USDA, told a *USA Today* reporter sometime in 1994 that he survived an asthma attack in a Costa Rican jungle by mixing a pinch of cayenne pepper in with some hot chocolate and slowly sipping it.

Bleeding Lungs

The following information appeared in an early Utah pioneer newspaper, *The Desert Weekly*. About 1882, a man named Thomas Child was helping haul rock for the construction of a Mormon meeting house in Provo, Utah, when he was formally greeted by another section hand. "I knew him, but could not place him." The man then reminded Child that they had previously met in Preston, England, where Child was serving a mission for his church. At that time, the man worked in the coal mines and suffered badly from a condition of bleeding lungs. Child advised him "to take a quarter of a teaspoonful of cayenne pepper every day for a week or two," which the man promptly started doing. The man finished by acknowledging that, "I am that man, and it cured me."

Bone Knitting

Take equal parts (three capsules or 20 drops each) of valerian root and cayenne pepper, along with some vitamin C (3,500 mg. daily) to dull the pain of breaks and fractures and help knit bones together more quickly.

Bursitis

Andrew Weil, M.D., a highly unconventional alternative practitioner and author of the best-selling *Spontaneous Healing*, has devised his own external skin rub for alleviating bursitis. He recommends taking some cayenne pepper (probably about a tablespoonful) and adding it to some rubbing alcohol (about a pint). The mixture should be left to set "at room temperature in a dark place until the alcohol is really bright red." After this it can be strained (optional) and used as an external rub. "It's great for arthritis and bursitis," Weil exclaimed.

Burning Sensation in Mouth

When your mouth is on fire from consuming too many chiles or cayenne pepper, the very best way to cool things off is by *slowly* drinking an eight-ounce glass of milk. Casein, the chief protein in milk, literally washes away the capsaicin, which binds to your taste buds and other receptors in your mouth.

Coughing

Jane Guiltinan, the chief medical officer at Bastyr University Natural Health Clinic in Seattle, always recommends the following remedy for getting rid of a nagging cough. Combine in a glass the juice of one-half of a lemon with one-half cup of warm water. Then stir in one tablespoon of salt and one-quarter teaspoon cayenne pepper. Gargle with it for as long and as deeply as you can tolerate it, before expectorating. *Don't swallow* it, though, she warns.

Food Poisoning

People who love eating raw sushi, oysters, or forms of *un-*dercooked seafood, run the risk of contracting a variety of harmful bacteria that can cause symptoms ranging from mild diarrhea to extremely dangerous blood poisoning. Some seafood markets and restaurants are also guilty of inadequate refrigeration of foods that should be kept cold at *all* times.

Cayenne pepper has come to the forefront as an easy solution to this potential health problem. At the American Society for Microbiology meeting in October 1993, scientists from the Louisiana State University Medical Center reported conducting a series of tests with certain noxious bacteria obtained from spoiled raw seafood.

They first added ketchup to each of the test tubes containing the bacteria. Nothing much happened. Lemon juice worked "moderately well," as did horseradish. But, much to their astonishment, straight hot sauce loaded with cayenne pepper killed all bacteria "in one minute flat!" Even when diluted to an insipid sixteen to one, the hot sauce still managed to kill all the bacteria in just under five minutes.

If lovers of sushi and sashimi ever needed a legitimate reason for using hot sauce, they have it now. In fact, sprinkling cayenne pepper over *any* raw or undercooked seafood is a good idea.

Hypothermia

A woman from San Jose, California has an idea for keeping her feet cozy warm in the wintertime. She empties the contents of a capsule of cayenne pepper into her hands and rubs it over each foot *before* putting her stockings and shoes on. She claims it keeps her feet from getting chilled. She recommends washing the hands thoroughly with soap and water after this procedure, however, so that no traces of cayenne are transferred to the face, nose or eyes where it can produce severe irritation. The same thing may be done with the hands before putting gloves on, but be sure *never* to touch your face with them until they've been thoroughly cleansed.

Influenza

Years ago while doing folk medicine research in the Yucatan Peninsula, I came down with a bad case of flu. I obtained some sour oranges common to that region of country, juiced them, and then added a pinch of cayenne pepper on the advice of an old female Maya *curandera* (folk healer). I drank, gargled and managed to swallow with great difficulty two large glasses of this horrid-tasting stuff. By the next morning, I was feeling 100 percent better.

Sometime later, I was a guest on the television religious program, "The 700 Club." The cohost, Ben Kinchlow, asked what his wife could take for her own severe bout with the flu. I mentioned the foregoing remedy and what it did for me. She tried it a day later and her flu symptoms disappeared in 24 hours!

I was intrigued by both of these incidents and decided to investigate the apparent synergy between capsaicin and ascorbic acid at further length. The results were nothing short of astonishing! Vitamin C works much better when some cayenne pepper accompanies it than when taken alone. The vitamin C remains in the body almost twice as long and works more powerfully than by itself. One capsule of cayenne for every 1,000 mg. of vitamin C is a good ratio. Eventually, I developed a special Super C with Cayenne for a leading supplement company, and it became one of their biggest sellers!

The *very best* combination I know, even more potent than synthetic antibiotics for clearing up infections of *any* kind, are garlic, goldenseal, cayenne pepper and vitamin C!

Insect Invasions

Most insects absolutely detest the pungent component in cayenne pepper. In a blender mix together two tablespoons of cayenne pepper, two cloves of garlic, four small white onions, and cook in one quart of water for a minute and a half. Strain and dilute in two gallons of water with two tablespoons of Ivory soap. Spray on plants to kill virtually all bugs.

Scatter a heavy and generous quantity of cayenne pepper around spring bulbs in flower to keep away squirrels and other pesky varmints. Nor will cats be inclined to dig in flower beds sprinkled with a lot of cayenne pepper. The cayenne won't hurt any of the flowers.

Kidney Problems

In 1870, an eastern gentleman by the name of DeWitt Clinton Pendery stepped off the stagecoach in what was then untamed Fort Worth, Texas. Local gunslingers jeered his elegant jim-dandy appearance as he stepped out onto the dusty street. One even went so far as to pull out his pistol and shoot the expensive tall silk hat right off Pendery's head.

Undaunted by this rude welcome, Pendery set up business there and was soon selling his own unique blends of spices to cafes, hotels, and citizenry near and far. He also sold his own special blend of cayenne pepper, cumin and oregano to local doctors, who claimed it worked marvels on inactive kidneys. Doctors also praised Pendery's mixture for alleviating the pain accompanying kidney stones that manage to travel through the system. Pendery's formula also stimulated the lymph glands and produced more beautiful-looking skin in those who took it regularly with whiskey or some other form of spirits.

Menstruation

Irregular menses may be corrected by taking two cayenne pepper capsules daily with a meal. There will often be less cramping and less bleeding with this regimen.

Morning Sickness

Two capsules each of catnip herb and cayenne pepper every morning should help to prevent morning sickness in women who are in the first trimester of their pregnancies.

Nose Bleeds

The following experience occurred in Salt Lake City, Utah in the latter part of 1892. An elderly lady was, according to Thomas Child, "taken with a severe attack of nasal bleeding." A doctor was called who plugged the nose, and put a cold stone to her back and in this uncomfortable position she was left.

"Having had time for reflection, she thought of . . . [using]

. . cayenne pepper. She had the stone and plug removed. Her nose bled profusely. She took one teaspoonful of cayenne and was immediately cured, said Child."

Pleurisy

Make a rub using equal parts of cayenne pepper, lobelia herb and slippery elm bark, all in powdered form. Next, mix in a little cod liver oil and stir thoroughly with a fork until a smooth paste is formed. (Be careful not to use too much oil or else the mixture will be too runny.) Apply this over the chest four times daily or about every three-and-a-half hours, cover with a piece of plastic sandwich wrap and then a clean flannel cloth.

Raynaud's Disease

This syndrome manifests itself as extreme sensitivity of the hands and fingers to cold as a result of spasm of the digital arteries. Other symptoms include blanching and numbness or pain of the fingers. One fellow who had been afflicted with this phenomenon for years switched from taking niacin (due to the flushing it caused) to 400 mg of cayenne pepper every day with food. When winter arrived, his hands remained toasty warm and stayed that way until springtime.

Sinusitis

A woman from Berkely Heights, New Jersey suffered from "a mild but stubborn sinusitis and bronchitis." She cured herself by "hastily lac[ing] a can of Campbell's [chicken soup] with . . . generous portions of [cayenne] pepper and garlic (about one-quarter teaspoon of each), simmered the brew to a perfect degree of piping hotness and drank it down."

Besides tasting good, it worked equally well. In less than five minutes, her incessant sneezing ceased, her "dry cough loosened and quieted" and her "stuffy nose began to breathe more freely."

Sore Muscles

To alleviate aching sore muscles, mix together the following ingredients: two crushed aspirin tablets; one-eighth teaspoon of eucalyptus oil or camphor; seven drops of wintergreen oil; one-eighth teaspoon of cayenne pepper powder; and a half-pint of rubbing alcohol. Shake contents thoroughly in a glass jar. Pour some directly onto sore muscles and rub some more between the palms of your hands. Then rub deeply into the skin by gently massaging the muscles with your fingers and fists.

Sore Throat
Here's a simple technique for getting rid of a sore throat. Stir one half-teaspoon of powdered cayenne pepper and one half-teaspoon of honey in one cup of grapefruit juice and gargle with it every hour on the hour. *Don't swallow* any of it!

Sprains
A wonderful liniment for sprains can be made by slowly simmering one tablespoon of cayenne pepper powder in one pint of apple cider vinegar. Bottle the unstrained liquid while it's still hot. When needed, reheat the liquid and soak an elastic cloth bandage (one that stretches) with some of this liquid and snugly wrap around the sprained limb. Note of caution: Prolonged application of a cayenne pepper liniment or rub to the skin may produce irritation, blisters or even burns. In the event that this occurs, cease using the liniment or rub and apply some aloe vera gel, extra virgin olive oil or cold-pressed flaxseed oil to the inflamed area.

Tonsillitis
A Nevada resident recommended one-half cup of hot water, one-fourth teaspoon of honey, a squirt of lemon juice and a pinch of cayenne pepper in the form of a periodic gargle administered several times throughout the day. It "works quickly" and eases suffering.

THE CHEMISTRY OF CAYENNE

By now you know that the chief component of cayenne pepper is, of course, capsaicin. This parent compound is "the most potent and predominant chemical entity found in the fruit of the plant" although there are "over 100 [other] distinct volatile compounds" which have been identified so far in the dark oleoresin extract. Capsaicin may occur as much as 0.5 to 1.5 percent in the fruit, with a series of similar compounds (homologous branched- and straight-chain alkyl vanillylamides), collectively known as the capsaicinoids. The content range can be as little as 0.1 to as much as 1.0 percent in capsicum plants. The capsaicinoid compounds include dihydrocapsaicin, nordihydrocapsaicin, homocapsaicin, and homodihydro-capsaicin.[39]

These five components in cayenne pepper act specifically upon the body by depleting stores of substance P from sensory neurons. This neuropeptide is an important transmitter of painful impulses from the periphery to the central nervous system. Noxious stimuli prompt release of substance P from sensory neurons distally toward the skin and joints and centrally into the spinal cord and brain stem. Release of substance P into distal tissues triggers a cascade of events associated with neurogenic inflammation.[40,41]

When a sensory neuron is subjected to purified capsaicin or any of the capsaicinoids, the neuron releases its supply of substance P and, upon repeated application, stops producing substance P. The neuron's ability to send a pain signal is diminished without substance P. After topical application, substance P stores revert to pretreatment levels and neuronal sensitivity returns to normal. Repeated administration of capsaicin is therefore necessary to control further sensations of pain.[42-44]

Substance P is also believed to be implicated in inflammatory bowel disease. Frequent consumption of cayenne pepper in small amounts may then prove to be very helpful in alleviating some of the pain associated with this problem. Not all varieties of capsicum will yield the same amounts of capsaicin, however. For example, *Capsicum frutescens* yields between 63.2–77.2 percent, *C. annuum* 36.9–59.1 percent and *C. pubescens* 25.5–36.3 percent.[45] So, it is important for consumers to know *which* type of capsicum they're getting if they expect to benefit from its capsaicin contents for problems of this nature.

Cayenne pepper is also a good source for some vitamins and minerals. Values for vitamin A can range from 3,350 I.U. for milder forms to 6,165 I.U. per gram of cayenne for some of the more pungent varieties. The discovery of vitamin C in some capsicums by Dr. Albert Szent-Györgyi has already been elaborated upon earlier in this text. And, as with other nutrients, content will vary: *C. frutescens* has 7.3 mg. per kilogram of fruit and *C. annuum* has 12 mg. per kg.[46] Vitamin E content is also significant: 100 grams of capsicum fruit yields anywhere from 3 to 10 mg of alpha-tocopherol. Some 16 amino acids have been reported in different capsicums, too.[47,48]

There are modest amounts of minerals as well, including calcium, phosphorus and potassium. A minute trace of cobalt (2 micrograms) has also been detected.[49]

Rating chiles according to their heat intensity is something of an imprecise science that relies largely on the perceptions of individual tasters. For decades chiles used to be scored according to their capsaicinoid content. This method of measurement was devised by a pharmacist named Wilbur Scoville. Most of the capsicums fall into a range from 0 to 300,000 Scoville Units (named after him). Green bell peppers obviously rate a fat zero since they lack capsaicinoids. On the other hand, the scotch bonnet from the Caribbean and the habañero from the Mexican Yucatan definitely go to the stratosphere in the heat they generate and earn their 300,000. Everything else is pretty much in between.

But over the last decade a new system has slowly evolved called the Official Chile Heat Scale, devised by writers of books and articles on chiles. It rates everything from a flat zero to a thermonuclear ten. So, bell peppers still languish at the bottom with zero, while the scotch bonnets and habañeros come in at a perfect ten. Everything else falls somewhere in between—the cayennes, for instance, come in around eight.

Two chile connoisseurs (euphemistically called chileheads) can sit down together and taste ten varieties of peppers and never find an agreement on a single one. The idea of "mine being hotter than yours" prevails throughout the brave but reckless eating world of chile aficionados. The only real hope of ever settling so many friendly disputes is scientifically . . . well, almost.

This is where a very expensive machine called a high-performance liquid chromatography unit (HPLC) comes into play. Freshly harvested chiles are oven-dried for several days. Afterwards they are ground into powder, mixed with a solvent and cooked for a few hours. That extracts the capsaiconoids from the powder. Then solid matter is carefully filtered out to yield an orange-colored liquid that is placed in glass vials and stored in a cupboard until needed. When testing occurs, a syringe is used to draw off some of the liquid from the vials and it is then injected into the HPLC machine, which consists of six metal boxes. Tubes and wires interconnect the different parts of this sophisticated piece of equipment. As the liquid runs continuously through the tubes, molecules get excited and special sensors observe what is present. In a short time a computer hooked up to the unit prints out a graph that resembles elongated mountain peaks between desert plains or some faraway planet.

Trained scientists can look at the machine's graph and detect which peaks are various capsaicinoids—one may be capsaicin while the other is dihydrocapsaicin. The particular graph I looked at one time happened to profile a type of güero chile known as Santa Fe Grande. But the same HPLC machine has *conclusively* proven which of all the chiles on the planet is the hottest little number in town. The scientific prize goes to the habañero from the Yucatan Peninsula, *Capsicum chinense*.

Each of the different capsaicinoids has its own unique behavioral characteristics. Some capsaicinoids produce a mellow, warming effect. Others sting immediately and dissipate very quickly, while a few more build slowly and then take forever to fade away. Some affect the front of the mouth, others the back of the tongue. Some yield a fruity, spicy quality. The most irritating one of all, though, is homodihydrocapsaicin. Unlike all of the other capsaicinoids, it has a noticeable aroma (it smells just like a chile) and it tastes sour like a pickle.

As noted earlier, a rule of thumb to remember in rating the many different chiles is this: the *smaller* in size, the *hotter* it's going to be when detonated within the mouth. This is because smaller chiles have a large amount of seeds and vein in contrast to larger chiles (which have smaller internal ribs and less seeds). These are the parts of a chile that contain up to 80 percent capsaicin. Knowing this little fact helps someone to reduce the heat intensity of chiles by simply removing both the veins and seeds.

Here is a list of some of the more popular chiles, their places of origin and their heat intensity according to the newer heat scale discussed earlier.[2]

Chiles	Origins	Heat
Aji	South America (Peru)	7–8
Amatista	South America	7
Anaheim (green)	Calif./Southwest	2–3
Anaheim (red)	Calif./Southwest	2–3
Chawa	Yucatan/Caribbean	3–4
Chilaca	Central Mexico	3–4
De Agua	Oaxaca, Mexico	4–5
Dutch (red)	Holland	6
Fiesta/Fips	Northern Mexico/Louisiana	6–8
Fresno (red)	Mexico/Calif./Southwest	6.5

Chiles	Origins	Heat
Güero	Northern Mexico/Southwest	4.5–6.5
Habánero	Yucatan/Caribbean	10
Huachinango	Central Mexico	5–6
Hungarian Cherry Pepper	Eastern Europe/Calif.	1–3
Hungarian Sweet Chile	Eastern Europe/Calif.	0–1
Jalapeño (red and green)	Mexico/Texas/Southwest	5.5
Jamaican Hot	Caribbean Islands	9
Korean	Korea/Japan/Calif.	6–7
Macho (green and red)	Oaxaca and Yucatan, Mexico	9–10
Manzana	Central America/Central Mexico	6–8
New Mexico (green)	Southwest	3–5
New Mexico (red)	Southwest	3–4
Peruvian	South America	7–8
Peter Pepper	Louisiana/Texas	7.5
Pimento	Southern U.S./Calif./Hungary/Spain	1
Poblano (green and red)	Central Mexico/Calif.	3
Rocotillo	South America	7–8
Santa Fe Grande	Northern Mexico/Southwest	6
Scotch Bonnet	Caribbean/Central America	9–10
Serrano	Mexico/Southwest	7
Tabasco	Louisiana/Central and South America	9
Tepin	Southwest/Central and South America	8
Thai	Southeast Asia/Calif.	7–8

RECOMMENDED READING

There is a great deal more information concerning the capsicums which interested readers are invited to peruse at their own leisure. I recommend the following publications as the best and most comprehensive on the subject:

Jean Andrews. *Peppers: The Domesticated Capsicums* (2nd Ed.) (Austin: University of Texas Press, 1995).

Mark Miller. *The Great Chile Book* (Berkeley: Ten Speed Press, 1991).

Susan Hazen-Hammond. *Chile Pepper Fever: Mine's Hotter Than Yours* (Stillwater, MN: Voyageur Press, Inc., 1993).

Chile Pepper magazine, 1227 West Magnolia, Fort Worth, TX 76104/1–888–SPICY HOT ($18.95 annually).

REFERENCES

1. "The hot side of chiles," *Science News* 134:41 (July 16, 1988).
2. Mark Miller, *The Great Chile Book* (Berkeley, CA: Ten Speed Press, 1991), pp. 12; 20–73.
3. P. M. D'Anghiera, *De orbo novo: The decades of the New World, or West India* (translated from the Latin by Rycharde Eden) (London: Hakluyt Society, 1904), 5:225–26.
4. Jean Andrews, *Peppers: The Domesticated Capsicums* (Austin: University of Texas Press, 1984), p. 8.
5. Fray Bernardino de Sahagún, *Florentine Codex* (Santa Fe: The School of American Research and The University of Utah, Monographs of the School of American Research, 1969), Book 6, Chapters 18–23 inclusive.
6. Richard Evans Schultes and Robert F. Raffauf, *The Healing Forest: Medicinal and Toxic Plants of the Northwest Amazonia* (Portland, OR: Dioscorides Press, 1990), p. 426.
7. Mark J. Plotkin, Ph.D., *Tales of a Shaman's Apprentice: An Ethnobotanist Searches for New Medicines in the Amazon Rain Forest* (New York: Viking, 1993).
8. F. C. Colpaert, et al., "Effects of capsaicin on inflammation and on the Substance P content of nervous tissues in rats with adjuvant arthritis," *Life Sciences* 32:1832 (1983).
9. Martin Lotz, et al., "Substance P activation of rheumatoid synoviocytes: Neural pathway in pathogenesis of arthritis," *Science* 235:893–895 (Feb. 20, 1987).
10. Jack Challem, "Hot peppers show hot health research," *NFM's Nutrition Science News* (November 1995), p. 42.
11. C. Vaughan, "Bowel-brain link may be key to diseases," *Science News* 133:324 (May 21, 1988).
12. "The Miracles of Cayenne Pepper," *The Lafayette Institute for Basic Research Health Discoveries Newsletter*, Issue 17, pp. 1–2 (1989).
13. S. Visudhiphan, et al., "The relationship between high fibrinolytic activity and daily capsicum ingestion in Thais," *American Journal of Clinical Nutrition* 35:1452–58 (1982).

14. P. Santicioli, et al., "Functional evidence for the existence of a capsaicin-sensitive innervation in the rat urinary bladder," *Journal of Pharmacy and Pharmacology* 38:446–51 (1986).

15. *Life Sciences* 56:1845–55 (April 21, 1995).

16. *Archives of Environmental Contamination & Toxicology* 28:248–58 (February 1995).

17. John Haydn Richards, "Cayenne, A Powerful Friend," *Bestways* (July 1978), p. 49.

18. M. T. Stock and K. Hunter, "Treat your head with something hot," *Chile Pepper* (May/June 1996), p. 32.

19. *West Indian Medical Journal* 31:194–197 (1982).

20. Anonymous, "Treatment of painful diabetic neuropathy with topical capsaicin. A multicenter, double-blind, vehicle-controlled study. The capsaicin study group," *Archives of Internal Medicine* 151:2225–2229 (November 1991).

21. Anonymous, "Effect of treatment with capsaicin on daily activities of patients with painful diabetic neuropathy. The capsaicin study group," *Diabetes Care* 15:159–165 (1992).

22. R. K. Campbell and D. E. Baker, "New drug update: Capsaicin," *Diabetes Education* 16:313–316 (1990).

23. M. T. Stock and K. Hunter, "The Healing Powers of Hot Pepper," *Chile Pepper* (May/June 1995), pp. 20–21.

24. K. Sambaiah and M. N. Satyanarayana, "Hypocholesterolemic effect of red pepper and capsaicin," *Indian Journal of Biochemistry* 18:898–99 (August 1980).

25. T. Kawada, et al., "Effects of capsaicin on lipid metabolism in rats fed a high fat diet," *Journal of Nutrition* 116:1271–78 (July 1986).

26. O. Hirayama, et al., *Lipids* 29:149–50 (February 1994). "Journal of Priddy Meeks," *Utah Historical Quarterly* 10:207 (1942).

27. B. M. Fusco, et al., *Pain* 59:321–25 (December 1994).

28. Nancy Benac, "Treatment of painful cluster headaches gives congress of doctors a migraine," *Salt Lake Tribune* (Thursday, July 4, 1991), p. A–6.

29. A. J. D'Alonzo, et al., *European Journal of Pharmacology* 272:269–78 (January 16, 1995).

30. D. Palevitch and L. E. Craker, "Nutritional and medical importance of red pepper (*Capsicum* ssp.)," *Journal of Herbs, Spices & Medicinal Plants* 3(2):67–70 (1995).

31. "Digestive De-tox and Ulcer Afterburners," *Chile Pepper* magazine (May/June 1995), p. 20.

32. Waykin Nopanitaya, "Effects of capsaicin in combination with diets

of varying protein content on the duodenal absorptive cells of the rat," *The American Journal of Digestive Diseases* 19:439;447 (May 1974).

33. Sheridan Warrick, "The Hungarian who wouldn't eat his peppers," *Hippocrates* (March/April 1988), p. 16.

34. "Red hot candy for cancer," *Chile Pepper* (July/August 1995), p. 23.

35. Joel E. Bernstein, M.D., et al., "Topical capsaicin treatment of chronic posttherapeutic neuralgia," *Journal of the American Academy of Dermatology* 21:265–70 (1989).

36. "A peppery preventive for pain," *Science News* 142:333 (November 14, 1992).

37. "Hot news for psoriasis," *Medical World News* (January 11, 1988).

38. "Cayenne and ulcers," *Herbalgram* 2(2):8 (Summer 1985).

39. Geoffrey A. Cordell and Oscar E. Araujo, "Capsaicin: Identification, nomenclature, and pharmacotherapy," *The Annals of Pharmacotherapy* 27:330–332 (March 1993).

40. T. Lewis, "The nocifensor system of nerves and its reactions," *British Medical Journal* 1:431–35;491–94(1937).

41. S. E. Carpenter and B. Lynn, "Vascular and sensory responses of human skin to mild injury after topical treatment with capsaicin," *British Journal of Pharmacology* 76:394–95 (1981).

42. R. Gamse, et al., "Differential effects of capsaicin on the content of somatostatin, substance P, and neurotensin in the nervous system of the rat," *Naunyn Schmiedebergs Arch. Pharmacol.* 217:140–48 (1981).

43. M. Fitzgerald, "Capsaicin and sensory neurons—a review," *Pain* 15:109–30 (1983).

44. R. H. LaMotte, et al., "Hypothesis for novel classes of chemoreceptors mediating chemogenic pain and itch"; *in* R. Dubner and G. F. Gebhart (Eds.), *Proceedings of the Fifth World Congress on Pain* (New York: Elsevier, 1988), pp. 529–35.

45. J. Jurenitsch, et al., "Identification of cultivated taxa of Capsicum: Taxonomy, anatomy and composition of pungent principle," *Chemical Abstracts* 91(35677g)313 (July 30, 1979).

46. Bep Oliver-Bever, *Medicinal Plants in Tropical West Africa* (Cambridge: University Press, 1986), p. 205.

47. V. S. Govindarajan, "Capsicum: Production, technology, chemistry, and quality. Part I: History, botany, cultivation, and primary processing," *CRC Critical Reviews in Food Science and Nutrition* 22(2):144–147 (1985).

48. V. S. Govindarajan and M. N. Sathyanarayana, "Capsicum—Production, technology, chemistry, and quality. Part V. Impact on physiol-

ogy, pharmacology, nutrition, and metabolism; structure, pungency, pain, and desensitization sequences," *Critical Reviews in Food Science and Nutrition* 29(6):435–74 (1991).

49. Alfredo Levy, "Microdetermination of cobalt in native Venezuelan foods," *Chemical Abstracts* 56:6420 (1962).

Writers' Walks
in Devon

Robert Hesketh

Bossiney Books · Exeter

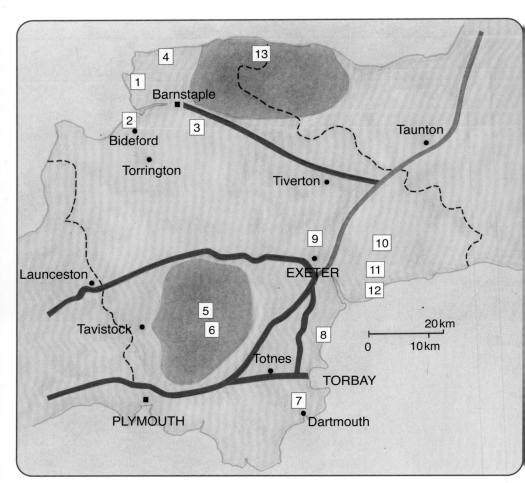

The approximate locations of the walks in this book

First published 2021 by
Bossiney Books Ltd, 68 Thorndale Courts, Whitycombe Way,
Exeter, EX4 2NY
www.bossineybooks.com
© 2021 Robert Hesketh All rights reserved
ISBN 978-1-906474-86-7

Acknowledgements
The maps are by Graham Hallowell except those on pages 8 and 14
which are by Nick Hawken
All photographs are by the author, www.roberthesketh.co.uk

Printed in Great Britain by R Booth Ltd, Penryn, Cornwall

Introduction

Exploring Devon's wonderful land and seascapes which have inspired generations of novelists and poets adds another dimension to reading them. Devon's scenery and unique character are inseparable from the writings of Agatha Christie, Jane Austen, Sir Arthur Conan Doyle, R D Blackmore, Rudyard Kipling, Henry Williamson and William Makepeace Thackeray. Several walks in this collection trace scenes from their work and places where they lived. Others visit the birthplaces of Sir Walter Raleigh, John Gay, Charles Kingsley and Samuel Taylor Coleridge, or, in the cases of George Eliot and Hilary Mantel, places that gave the authors special delight.

Ranging from 4.7 km (3 miles) up to 12.3 km (7 1/2 miles), these walks are as diverse as the writers associated with them, so the time needed will vary too – but why hurry? Devon is here to be enjoyed.

Footwear, clothing and extras

Walking is a pleasure throughout the seasons so long as you're prepared. There will be some mud at most times of the year and perhaps a lot of mud and puddles in winter. Walking boots are ideal, but sandals inadequate, whilst Wellingtons don't breathe or provide ankle support. Devon's weather can change suddenly and it most certainly rains, so it's wise to bring extra layers of clothing as well as a waterproof. On some paths there may be gorse or nettles, therefore trousers are preferable to shorts, especially as they provide some protection against ticks which may carry Lyme disease. If a tick does attach itself to you, remove it promptly and carefully with tweezers.

Drinking water is a must – dehydration causes tiredness. I recommend a walking pole or stick and a mobile phone and GPS device if you have them. The sketch maps in this book are just that – sketches. You may want to carry the relevant OS Explorer for extra information.

The countryside

Walking is safe and healthy exercise, but please watch out for unfenced cliffs, uneven and waterlogged ground. Despite many pressures on their livelihoods, farmers are still trying to make a living from the land you will pass through. Please respect their livestock and leave gates closed or open as you find them. It is essential to keep dogs under control, especially during the lambing and bird nesting season.

Finally, please respect the privacy of writers and those who now live in their former homes when you pass by.

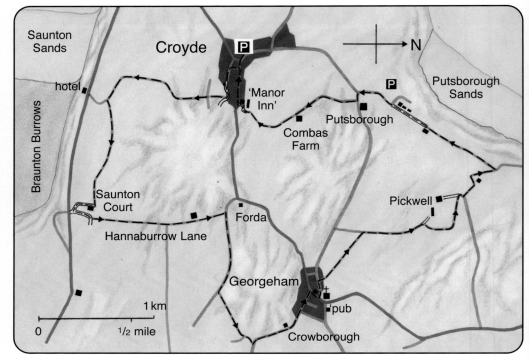

Walk 1 Georgeham and Henry Williamson

Distance; 11.7km (7¹/₄ miles)   Duration: 4 hours
Character: This beautiful route offers a variety of scenery, from surf-washed sands and rocky cliffs to flower-strewn paths and green fields and two attractive villages noted for their thatched buildings.

Start from Croyde's Village Hall car park. Turn right, then left 20m ahead. After a further 40m turn right across the stream and follow Watery Lane to the top. Turn left and continue as the lane becomes a track, PUBLIC BRIDLEWAY. Walk uphill. Just 20m beyond a multi-path junction turn right (PUBLIC FOOTPATH) at a gate.

Continue ahead (SAUNTON) at the next footpath junction, following an enclosed path to an open field. Continue diagonally right uphill, SAUNTON. Enjoy the view of Croyde and Baggy Point. Walk ahead over the crest of the hill for another splendid view – Braunton Burrows and Saunton Sands with the Taw/Torridge estuary in the background.

Follow the path diagonally left and downhill to a junction. Keep left, SAUNTON AVOIDING AMENITIES. Walk through two fields and follow the track gently downhill, passing to the right of Saunton Court, a late medieval manor house remodelled by Lutyens in 1932.

4

The track forks. Turn sharp left, PRIVATE LANE. This soon joins a grassy path (PUBLIC BRIDLEWAY) rich with wildflowers. Continue uphill to the crest, then downhill, BRIDLEWAY. Descend to a tarmac lane and turn right. Bear left after 550 m, PUBLIC FOOTPATH. This leads across a field, over a stile and into an enclosed path. Keep left when the path divides. Turn left onto the lane and continue to a T-junction by the village shop. Turn right, then left at the Kings Arms.

Walk downhill past the church – Henry Williamson's grave is by the west tower. Continue past cottages bearing blue plaques showing Williamson lived in them. After a further 50 m, turn right up a footpath, which follows an enclosed track then turns left through a series of well-signed fields and gates.

Turn right at the lane. Follow the lane when it diverts around Pickwell Manor Farm to Pickwell Cross. Follow the lane right, then only 25 m ahead turn left, PUBLIC FOOTPATH. At the next waymark, bear left and downhill, but after 50 m turn right at the waymark. This dogleg avoids passing in front of a wooden house. The footpath leads gently downhill to a gate, then more steeply to a second gate.

Turn left onto the signed Coast Path. Follow the Coast Path acorn signs, ignoring side turnings. On reaching the lane continue ahead, COAST PATH. However, do not take the next Coast Path turning. Continue on the tarmac lane. Don't take the lane for Croyde, but walk ahead, PUTSBOROUGH GEORGEHAM.

Turn right at the pond by Putsborough Manor. Continue ahead at Combas Farm. Reaching Croyde, follow the lane to the right, then turn right past the front of the Manor Inn and follow the lane (which can be quite busy so take care) to the start.

5

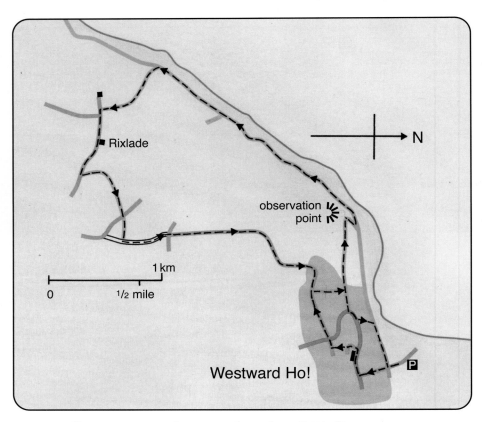

Rixlade

observation
point

Westward Ho!

1 km

0   1/2 mile

N

Walk 2   Westward Ho! and Rudyard Kipling

Distance: 10.7 km (6 3/4 miles)   Time: 3 1/2 hours

*Character: A pleasing mix of coastpath, footpaths and quiet lanes,
this walk includes sweeping views of the dramatic North Devon coast.
En route is Kipling's old school and Kipling Tors, where the author and
his school friends repaired to smoke pipes and discuss books as described
in 'Stalky and Co'. Parts muddy after rain. A few short, steep slopes.*

Start from the Pebbleridge Road car park, signed NORTHAM BURROWS.
Turn left (away from the sea) up PEBBLERIDGE ROAD to a junction.
Continue up AVON LANE. Turn right at the T-junction. On the left
above the road is a long terrace, formerly the United Services College,
where Kipling was educated from 1878 to 1882, as a plaque at the foot
of the steps half-way along declares.

Bear next left up KINGSLEY ROAD. Turn sharp left up KIPLING
TERRACE. Turn sharp right up steps, PUBLIC FOOTPATH. At the top of

the steps continue ahead. Turn left and uphill at the T junction. At the next junction, turn right into BAY VIEW ROAD and cross STANWELL HILL into CORNBOROUGH ROAD.

Turn right through a gate, PUBLIC FOOTPATH. Reaching a four-way path junction, turn left and uphill along a high level path. Keep left at the next junction, to an early 20th century lookout with a viewing table and a plaque about Kipling.

Retrace your steps to the junction. Continue steeply downhill. Turn left onto the Coast Path and follow it for the next 2.2 km (1 1/2 miles).

Ignore the PUBLIC FOOTPATH ABBOTSHAM. Continue. Cross a footbridge and turn left at a gate up a footpath.

Meeting a lane, continue ahead at the junction past Rixlade. Turn left, PUBLIC FOOTPATH. Cross a stile on the right and follow the right field edge. Continue over a footbridge to a lane. Turn right, then left after 60 m. Turn left into a track. Continue to a lane. Walk ahead, then right (CORNBOROUGH) and follow the lane for 1.6 km (1 mile).

Turn left, PUBLIC FOOTPATH (the same path used earlier in the walk). Continue to the four-way footpath junction and turn right. Follow the zig-zag path down to a junction and turn right. Continue to a road. Turn left and follow the road as it curves right.

Turn left (PUBLIC FOOTPATH) opposite a church. Reaching the sea wall, turn right by the Kipling signboard and follow it to a signpost. Bear right, CAR PARK. Turn left into Pebbleridge Road to the start.

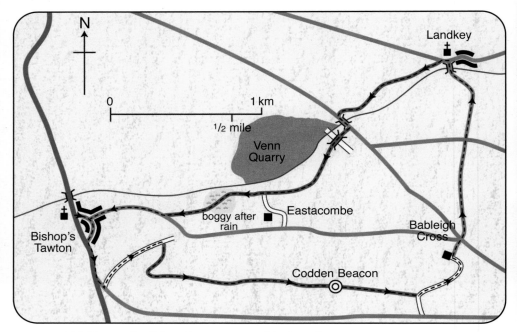

Walk 3 Codden Beacon and John Gay

Distance: 8 km (5 miles)   Time: 2 1/2 hours

Character: Footpaths and quiet country lanes. The circuit includes Codden Beacon (189 m, 620 ft), a magnificent viewpoint, as well as two interesting villages. One short but very steep ascent.

Park next to Bishop's Tawton parish church, noted for its crocketed octagonal spire, unique in Devon, and for the sanctuary ring set in its door. Turn right from the church, walk up the main road and bear left into Village Street, past the 15th century Chichester Arms.

Turn left to rejoin the main road and after 150 m turn left into the lane signed COBBATON AND CHITTLEHAMPTON. Immediately, turn left. Ignore the track. Take the PUBLIC FOOTPATH up steps. The path climbs steeply and then continues with a gentler gradient. Keep the wire fence on your right and continue to Codden Beacon, crowned with a memorial to Caroline, wife of former Liberal leader and local MP, Jeremy Thorpe.

Use the directional compass on the monument to spot landmarks, then take the downhill path to the east. At a gate this joins a broad track just beyond a small car park. At a junction of tracks turn sharp left, taking the track downhill between hedges to a lane; this bears

8

right in front of Pitt Farm, and on to Bableigh Cross. Take the second lane on the left, signed LANDKEY.

Landkey church has a typically Devonian tower with battlements and gargoyles. Bear left (or right if you want to explore the village or visit the Castle Inn) and take the lane for Barnstaple. After 80 m, turn left at the Tarka Trail footpath sign. Go through two gates and follow a well-beaten path through a wood by a brook.

At a gate turn left onto the lane and cross the bridge. Follow the Tarka Trail waymarks, turning right 50 m beyond the bridge. The path leads around Venn Quarries and over an arched bridge. Continue along the footpath.

Turn right through a small gate and continue along the trail through a pair of gates and along the woodland edge by a brook. (This section becomes boggy after heavy rain: you can divert left at the pair of gates, up a grassy then tarmac track to the lane, then turn right along the lane back to Bishop's Tawton.) Follow the field edge from the next gate to the far field corner, where the next gate is half hidden, some 30 m up the slope to your left.

Cut diagonally across the next field in line with the telegraph pole ahead. Exit at the top corner and continue in the same line across a further field to a gate. Turn right and follow the lane back to Bishop's Tawton.

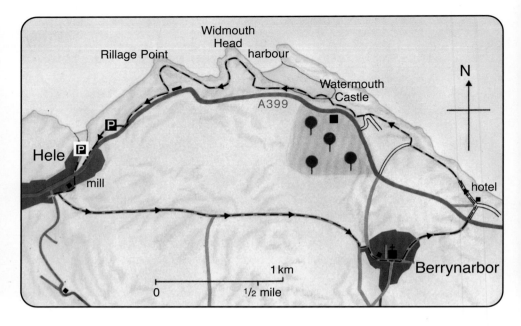

Walk 4   Hele, Berrynarbor and 'George Eliot'

Distance: 9.7 km (6 miles)   Time: 3 hours
Character: This moderately demanding route includes five sharp but
fairly short ascents, and much of interest, including lanes and paths
rich with wild flowers and some of North Devon's most spectacular
coastal views. George Eliot wrote of her visit to Ilfracombe with George
Henry Lewes in 1856: 'We are enchanted with Ilfracombe. I really think
it is the loveliest sea-place I ever saw, from the combination of fine
rocky coast with exquisite inland scenery.'

Turn left out of Hele car park. Cross the main road and take the
PUBLIC FOOTPATH opposite. This leads through the grounds of Hele
Mill, which is run as a working watermill with a tea garden and
handicrafts.

Reaching a tarmac lane (Old Berrynarbor Road), turn left and
follow it uphill for 1.2 km (3/4 mile). Ignore the lane on the right and
continue ahead. Follow the lane downhill, passing under a bridge and
into Berrynarbor. At a junction turn left, BERRYNARBOR. Turn right at
a second junction, BERRYNARBOR. Continue uphill past the Old Globe,
an historic inn with exposed beams, stone fireplaces and a collection
of antiques, to the church.

10

From the church – worth visiting for its impressive tower, Norman font and monuments – walk ahead (COMBE MARTIN) following Barton Lane as it curves left and uphill. Continue to the main road. Cross carefully and walk ahead (COAST PATH) to the entrance of Sandy Cove Hotel.

Turn left, then immediately bear right on OLD COAST ROAD. The road soon becomes a stony track, leading through trees. Just before it joins a tarmac lane, turn right, COAST PATH. Follow the beaten path to the right of the campsite, onto a tarmac track, then ahead to the main road as signed.

Turn right along the pavement, then into an enclosed path. Rejoin the pavement and turn almost immediately right (COAST PATH) opposite Watermouth Castle – or divert down the tarmac track to the Boat Café (a converted boat called *Teacup*) overlooking the harbour. Except for an hour either side of some high tides, when walkers must follow the pavement for 150 m, it is possible to cut across the muddy sand, then turn left up steps, COAST PATH.

Happily, the Coast Path soon diverges from the pavement. Magnificent views of Watermouth open up, with a series of high cliffs beyond, especially as the path climbs Widmouth Head.

Keep following COAST PATH signs. After Rillage Point the path again runs parallel to the road. Walk through the car park and picnic area, then rejoin the road, following the pavement downhill to the start.

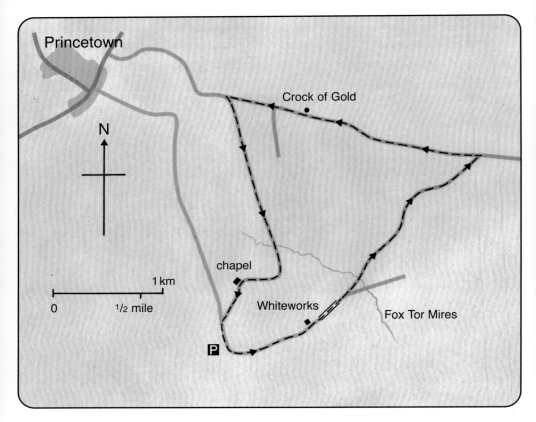

Walk 5 Whiteworks and Conan Doyle

Distance: 8.6 km (5 1/2 miles)   Time: 3 hours

Character: This stimulating walk offers panoramic views of central Dartmoor, including Foxtor Mires, the inspiration for Conan Doyle's 'Grimpen Mire' in 'The Hound of the Baskervilles'. Much of the route is on tracks and paths, but there is a section of open moor over rough, damp ground and a slightly tricky stream crossing. Walking boots, map and compass needed. Do not attempt after heavy rain.

Directions to the start: Take the TOR ROYAL turning by the Fox Tor Café in Princetown. Continue 550 m beyond Tor Royal to the parking area at SX 604708.

Turn right down the lane. Continue past Whiteworks – Foxtor Mires are on your right. At the end of the lane, continue ahead on a rough track. Go through a gate and follow the bridleway ahead. At a fork (not marked on the OS map) keep left on a north-easterly course.

12

Cross the stream ahead with care. Follow the path to the top of the ridge. Over on the left is an impressive cairn, ahead a panorama studded with tors. Continue ahead, keeping to the same north-easterly course over open ground to strike a broad, clear track, the 'Conchies Road', built during WW1 by conscientious objectors incarcerated at Dartmoor Prison for refusing military service.

Turn left and follow the track towards the TV mast on North Hessary Tor. Look out for the Crock of Gold on the right – a Bronze Age cist, a rectangular burial chamber with nearby stones marking the retaining stone circle. Continue ahead. Ignore the first track left. Continue to a track junction.

Turn sharp left and follow the clear track ahead. Ignore side turnings. Continue ahead with the wall on your right, crossing the stream by a footbridge. Continue to a stile set up on a stone wall.

Turn right over the stile. Follow the path parallel to the leat. Turn left as signed over a clapper bridge. Follow the path right by the chapel. Continue ahead at the track junction for 100 m. Turn left onto the tarred track. Continue to the start.

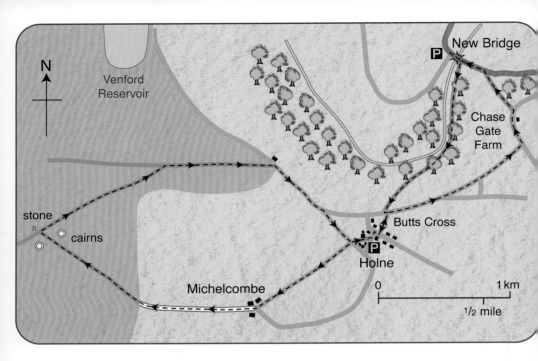

Walk 6 Holne and New Bridge, Charles Kingsley

Distance: 6.8km (4¹/₄ miles) or 10.8km (6³/₄ miles)
Time: 2¹/₄ hours or 3¹/₂ hours.

Character: A figure of eight walk with magnificent moorland views. We start from Holne, noted for its historic church and Church House Inn. The optional second loop includes medieval New Bridge and a beautiful riverside path. One longish ascent and descent on each loop.

Turn right out of Holne village car park to view the 14th century Church House Inn and the church. Probably first built in the 13th century, it was enlarged, like many Devon churches, in the 15th century and has a splendid rood screen.

From the church porch, head to the far top corner of the churchyard and leave by a kissing gate. Continue to a lane. Take the lane ahead, MICHELCOMBE.

Reaching the hamlet, bear right, NO THROUGH ROAD BRIDLEWAY ONLY. Continue ahead at the next path junction and follow the path uphill to the moor gate. Continue ahead and uphill on the same NW course. The path crosses a leat and a dry water channel (once the Wheal Emma leat). Continue steadily uphill towards the summit.

When you see two barrows (prehistoric burial mounds marked as 'cairns' on the map), cross over.

Now make a 90° turn right from the path by which you arrived and walk NE downhill on the beaten path, ignoring side turnings. On reaching a stony track, turn east (right) and walk down to a lane.

Turn right and follow the lane downhill. Fork right at the next junction, SCORRITON. Continue to the Michelcombe turn. Retrace your steps to the start.

For the second loop, turn right out of the car park and past the Church House Inn. Cross the lane and continue ahead, ASHBURTON PRINCETOWN. Reaching BUTTS CROSS, turn right, ASHBURTON PRINCE-TOWN. Ignore the turning right and continue ahead. Keep left at the next junction and left at Stony Post Cross. Continue past Chase Gate Farm for 100 m. Take the footpath left, COUNTY ROAD NEW BRIDGE. Cross a stile and follow the right field edge downhill.

Cross another stile. Turn left down the lane to see New Bridge. Recross the bridge and turn right over a footbridge, PUBLIC FOOTPATH. Broad and well-surfaced, it follows the river. Reaching a fork, turn left, FOOTPATH HOLNE. Follow the path uphill through fields via gates and stiles. Reaching a lane turn left and almost immediately right at Butts Cross. Retrace your steps to the start.

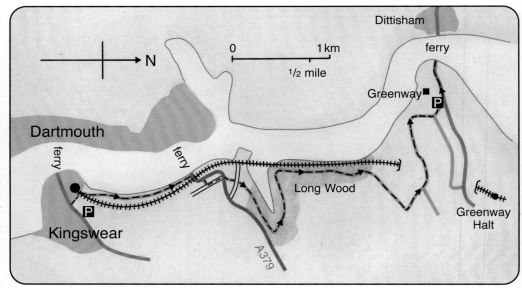

Walk 7 Kingswear to Greenway, and Agatha Christie

Distance: 6.3km (4 miles)   Time: 2 hours

Character: This beautiful walk follows the Dart Valley Trail through woods and fields beside the sinuous river and sections of the steam railway, with fine views of Dartmouth and Dittisham and over the hills to Dartmoor. There is an optional visit to Agatha Christie's summer home, Greenway, and its lovely gardens (National Trust).

Return by ferries Greenway/Dartmouth and Dartmouth/Kingswear (01803 882811) or steam train Greenway Halt/Kingswear (01803 555872). Please check timetables and book in advance.

Start from the Kingswear Marina car park. Turn right out of the car park. Turn right over the footbridge, which gives a fine view of Kingswear station. Follow the marked footpath ahead, parallel to the railway as far as the Higher Ferry.

Turn right over the level crossing. Follow the road uphill. Turn right up steps at a fingerpost, PERMISSIVE PATH DART VALLEY TRAIL.

Turn left at the top of the path and follow the drive. Cross the road carefully and follow the trail down steps. Cross a lane. Continue uphill into Long Wood to the head of a creek. Follow the path left and around the creek as far as the Higher Ferry.

The path continues north parallel to the river. Continue as the path

zig-zags uphill. When the path divides, keep right and uphill, DART VALLEY TRAIL. Leave Long Wood and continue ahead.

Reaching a path junction, turn left, GREENWAY GARDENS. Follow the path right, then left past Maypool. A superb view of the Dart appears as you enter Greenway.

Turn right, GREENWAY GARDENS. Turn left at the next fingerpost (or turn right and follow the path to Greenway Halt for the Dart Valley Railway, 700 m). Follow the path steeply downhill to the car park.

Either turn left to visit Greenway House and Gardens (admission charge or National Trust membership) or turn right for the ferry or train. Turn left onto the lane (or right for the railway 700 m). Continue to the ferry steps, where there is a café.

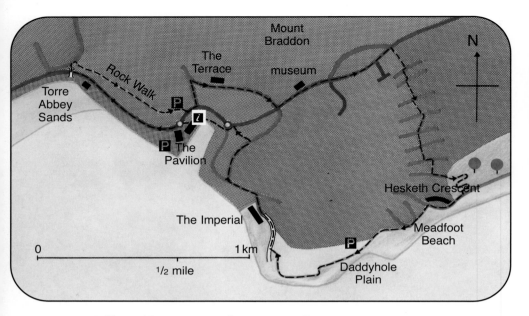

Walk 8 Torquay and many authors

Distance: 6 km (3³/₄ miles)   Time: 1³/₄ hours

Character: Savour Torquay's handsome nineteenth century architecture and enjoy magnificent views over Torbay, but be prepared for some very stiff climbs via steps. Torquay was Agatha Christie's birthplace, Disraeli and Kipling had houses here, and Kingsley and others came for health reasons.

Start from the Pavilion. Agatha Christie's memorial bust (1990) is opposite in Palk Street. Walk away from the harbour, past the Princess Theatre and Princess Pier. Cross the road by a pedestrian bridge, turn right up Shedden Hill and right again after 200 m into Rock Walk, which leads back along the edge of the cliff.

Follow steps down to the main road. Turn left across the entrance of a multi-storey car park, then left again up Fleet Street. Try to imagine it as it was 250 years ago, as a picturesque and unspoilt stream with a mill! After 100 m turn sharp right up a narrower street, with St John's church high above on the left. Continue along The Terrace, first built for naval officers during the Napoleonic Wars.

Turn left at the traffic light and climb uphill to the Museum, which has a special Agatha Christie Gallery. Continue around the S bend, past many luxurious Victorian villas.

18

About 100 m beyond LISBURNE SQUARE turn right into a path opposite OLD TORWOOD ROAD and start a serious climb.

Cross three roads (in each case right and immediately left) and at the fourth (the summit!), bear slightly right beside 'Haldon Rise' down a lane with stone walls on either side. Cross HIGHER LINCOMBE ROAD and descend via the footpath. Cross another road (right, then left) then at the next road turn left and after 50 m right.

At the next road turn left. This time continue to its end and follow a footpath into the woods. After 100 m keep right. Follow the zig-zag path down to Meadfoot Beach, where Agatha came to swim. Turn right along the road and left up steps opposite splendid Hesketh Crescent, CAR PARK DADDYHOLE PLAIN. Cross the car park. Follow the Coast Path up a slope and more steps. At the far end of Daddyhole Plain the National Coastwatch has a small visitor centre. Walk ahead into ROCK END WALK (part of the Coast Path). Continue via steps and changes of direction until you reach a T junction with a broad tarmac path. Turn right past Peaked Tor Cove and cross the entrance of The Imperial hotel.

Turn left down the road, then bear right along PARKHILL ROAD. Opposite Vane Hill House, turn left down steps to the Strand. Cross the back of the harbour. Turn left along VAUGHAN PARADE, past the Tourist Information Centre to the Pavilion.

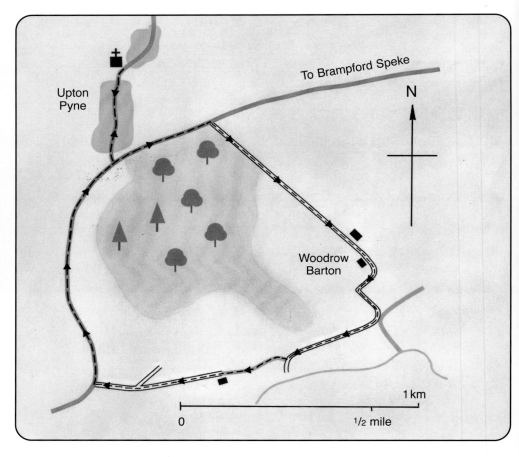

Walk 9   Upton Pyne and Jane Austen

Distance: 5.1 km (3 1/4 miles)   Time: 1 3/4 hours
Character: A pleasant walk by country lanes and field paths, with fine views of the Exe Valley and rolling hills beyond.

Start at Upton Pyne, thought to be the inspiration for the fictional village of Barton in 'Sense and Sensibility'. Like Barton, Upton Pyne is 'four miles northward of Exeter' and set amidst 'high hills which rise behind it ... some of which are open downs, the others cultivated and woody.' Muddy in parts. Some moderate ups and downs.

Start from the small square in front of Upton Pyne's medieval church or park carefully nearby. In the novel, Elinor and Edward are married on an autumn day at Barton church and one may readily imagine the

20

scene, see photo above. Turn right and walk uphill along the main street to the BRAMPFORD SPEKE junction.

Turn left and follow the lane. Where New Wood ends on the right, turn right (PUBLIC BRIDLEWAY) with the wood on your right. Continue ahead along a broad track. Walk ahead at a track junction. The signed path leads past sheds on your left and Woodrow Barton on your right. Author Anne-Marie Edwards (*In the Footsteps of Jane Austen*) identifies cottages at Woodrow Barton as the likely model of Jane Austen's 'Barton Cottage', which the Dashwoods rented and from where 'The prospect…commanded the whole of the valley and reached into the countryside beyond.'

Follow the track as it bends right. Turn right at a track junction, PUBLIC FOOTPATH. When the track forks, keep ahead (left). Leave the track when it bends left to a weir. Continue ahead through a small woodland gate, PUBLIC FOOTPATH. Follow the footpath through another gate and along the field edge. The path continues around farm buildings and along a farm track.

Reaching the lane by Little Pyne House, turn right and uphill to the Brampford Speke junction. Retrace your steps to the start.

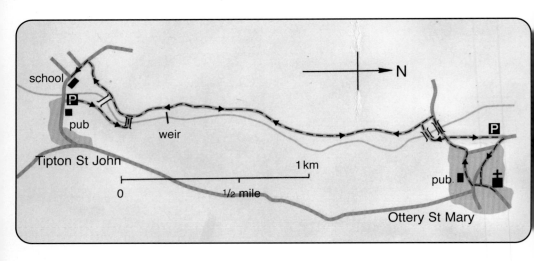

Walk 10 Ottery St Mary, Coleridge and Thackeray

Distance: 10 km (6 1/4 miles)   Time: 3 1/4 hours

Character: This gentle and attractive riverbank walk links the pretty village of Tipton St John with historic Ottery St Mary, where Samuel Taylor Coleridge was born in 1772 and spent his early childhood. William Makepeace Thackeray lived for some time near the town. Mainly level, parts may be muddy after rain.

Start from Ottery's Canaan Way car park. Walk through the car park and cross the road ahead, signed HONITON. Continue along the street. Branch slightly left into the narrow SADDLERS LANE and left again into SILVER STREET. Walk uphill to visit the magnificent church, noted for its fan vaulting and medieval clock. There is a large plaque to Coleridge in the churchyard wall, right of the church steps.

Retrace your steps down SILVER STREET. Continue to the Square. Cross to the Volunteer Inn and turn right down MILL STREET. Bear left at CANAAN WAY. Bear left by Albert Close into the COLERIDGE LINK FOOTPATH. Turn right over the footbridge ahead.

Simply turn left and follow the riverbank path south for the next 3 km, often following or very close to the former Sidmouth Junction to Exmouth branch railway (1874 to 1967). Look out for wildfowl, including mallards and egrets, plus signs of otters and the recently re-introduced beavers. On the way is a large weir, which powered the now defunct mill via a leat that now powers a generator with an Archimedes Screw.

22

Continue along the west bank, past the footbridge and the arched brick bridge ahead. Continue to a metal gate and turn right along the footpath. Turn left along the lane, past a junction on the right, the school and over the bridge.

Turn left across the car park. Continue across the playing field. Leave at the top right corner. Follow the east bank upstream to the bridge by the former mill and cross over.

Retrace your steps up the west bank. Do not cross the footbridge. Continue to the road. Turn right over St Saviour's Bridge (1851) and almost immediately left, PUBLIC FOOTPATH. Follow this footpath behind restored Otter Mill. Note the unusual tumbling weir. Continue along the footpath to the start.

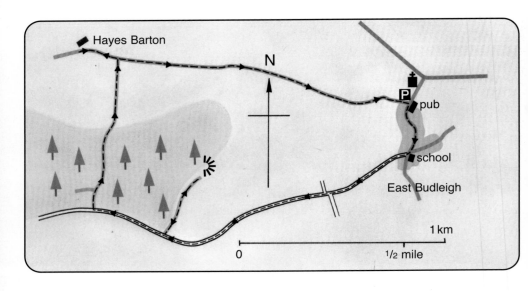

Walk 11   East Budleigh and Sir Walter Raleigh

Distance: 4.7 km (3 miles)   Time: 1 1/2 hours

Character: This fairly gentle walk includes fine views of the East Devon coast and countryside. It begins at the attractive village of East Budleigh, which has many cob and thatch buildings, including the Sir Walter Raleigh Inn – a grade II listed 16th century building with several local period photographs. En route are Hayes Barton, a substantial cob farmhouse where Sir Walter was born in 1552 ,and East Budleigh church, which has Raleigh's portrait, a 16th century memorial to Joan Raleigh and a bench end with the Raleigh coat of arms.

Start at East Budleigh's signed free car park. Divert up CHURCH LANE to see the church. Retrace your steps to the car park and turn left then right opposite the Sir Walter Raleigh Inn. Follow the main street.

Turn right opposite Drake's School and walk ahead past Wynard's Farm onto Hayeswood Lane, an attractive green lane worn deep into the underlying rock. Ignore the tracks left and right and continue uphill. Divert right at a path junction (PUBLIC FOOTPATH) for 200 m to enjoy a splendid view over East Budleigh to Peak Hill, the East Devon coast and on into Dorset as far as Portland Bill. Retrace your steps to the path junction and turn right.

Turn right again at a metal gate, PUBLIC FOOTPATH. Follow the path uphill into Hayes Wood. Continue ahead at a junction of paths. Keep

right at the next junction. Walk past Hayeswood Cottage and follow the track ahead.

Reaching Hayes Lane, divert left to see Hayes Barton. Please note, Hayes Barton is private, but may be viewed from the road. Please respect the owners' privacy.

Turn around and follow Hayes Lane back to the start.

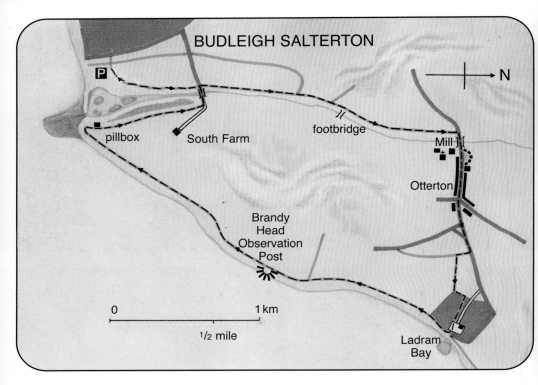

Walk 12 Budleigh Salterton and Hilary Mantel

Distance: 11.6 km (7¹/₄ miles)   Time: 3¹/₂ hours

Character: Starting by Budleigh's pebble beach, this walk combines coast and riverbank paths with superb views of the Jurassic Coast and birdwatching on the Otter Estuary Nature Reserve. Halfway is Otterton, with its working watermill and cob and thatch houses. Easy walking, no really steep slopes. Special note: Take binoculars.

Start from Budleigh's Lime Kiln car park, SY072820. Leave at the far right corner along a gravelled footpath. Watch for birds on the estuary and meadows. You may also see trout and mullet in the river, or spot recently introduced beavers.

Reaching a bridge, continue ahead (PUBLIC FOOTPATH OTTERTON) on the same bank. Pass a metal footbridge. Turn right to Otterton Mill, which still grinds flour with water powered machinery. It also has a gallery, artists' workshops and a café.

Walk on past the King's Arms and a line of 16th/17th century cottages and farmhouses with characteristically Devonian lateral

26

chimneystacks. When the road bends left, walk ahead up BELL STREET LEADING TO LADRAM BAY. Continue uphill. Ignore the tarmac lanes on the right, then near the top of the slope turn right along a track, PUBLIC WAY. Only 35 m ahead, turn left, LADRAM BAY. The track becomes a path and leads into Ladram Bay holiday centre. Continue ahead, signed COAST PATH, then keep right for BUDLEIGH SALTERTON.

You will get an arresting view of Ladram Bay's rock stacks with High Peak behind. These are part of a chain of New Red Sandstones, between 180 and 225 million years old, that stretches from Torbay to east of Sidmouth. On a clear day the view extends along the Dorset coast to Portland Bill.

Follow the undulating cliff path to Brandy Head – a name recalling Devon's long smuggling traditions – and its restored WW2 observation post. Continue to the Otter estuary. Seabirds wheel and call below. They nest in ledges and crevices. Don't go too close to the cliff edge – it's a sheer drop.

Follow the Coast Path as it turns upriver by a WW2 pillbox, now maintained as a winter bat roost. Indeed, there are bat boxes in the trees along the riverbank, where a hide offers excellent opportunities to watch the birds. In medieval times, before the shingle ridge formed, the Otter was navigable as far as Otterton. The saltpans (hence Budleigh Salterton) were worked where the rich mudflats are now.

Turn left at South Farm. Follow the lane ahead over the bridge. Turn left BUDLEIGH SALTERTON and retrace your steps to the start.

Walk 13 The Doone Valley and R D Blackmore

Character: This pleasant there-and-back stroll along Exmoor's 'Doone Valley' takes you to the robbers' lair of the dastardly Doone clan. The scenery is beautiful, though (as he admitted) not as hugely dramatic as R D Blackmore described.

Start from Lorna Doone Farm at Malmsmead with its parking and refreshments. Take LANE LEADING TO PUBLIC FOOTPATH DOONE VALLEY (or pay 50p and use the riverbank path). After 250m, bear left PUBLIC BRIDLEWAY BADGWORTHY WATER.

Continue for 3.5km (2¼ miles) along the footpath beside the river Barle. Just beyond the sign BRENDON COMMON LARKBARROW, the path curves right. On the left is an abandoned medieval village. Its bracken-covered ruins are typical of local longhouses, with one room for the farmer's family and one for the animals. It has decayed greatly since Blackmore wrote *Lorna Doone* in 1869 – you need some imagination to see the Doones in all their wicked splendour.

Jane Austen (1775-1817)

Jane Austen and her family spent at least two summers in Devon, at Sidmouth for three months in 1801 and in Dawlish then Teignmouth the following year. All three towns, but especially Sidmouth, are worth exploring for their buildings from that period. Little detail of these holidays is known, but her father had social contacts among the clergy, and it is probable that the family made visits in the area, including to Upton Pyne. It is possible that our walk is in part that taken by Marianne and Margaret in *Sense and Sensibility* – though Elinor would surely doubt it!

Richard Doddridge Blackmore (1825-1900)

R D Blackmore was the author of *Lorna Doone* (1869), which he did not think his best novel, but which is the only one remembered today. Blackmore's family were from Devon: his father was a curate in Berkshire at the time of his birth, but his mother soon died, and an aunt looked after him till he was seven. He spent much of his childhood in various parts of Devon, and was educated at Blundell's School in Tiverton. His grandfather was rector of Oare from 1809, and then of Combe Martin also, and he had fond memories both of his grandfather and the Exmoor landscape.

Agatha Christie (1890-1976)

Agatha Christie née Miller was born in Torquay, where there are many places associated with her. In 1938 she and her husband Max Mallowan purchased Greenway house, overlooking the Dart, and spent their holidays there. The house is now owned by the National Trust and, with its gardens, is open to the public.

Samuel Taylor Coleridge (1772-1834)

Coleridge was born at Ottery St Mary, where his father was vicar, and also headmaster of the Free Grammar School. Samuel was the youngest of 13 children. His father died when he was eight, and Coleridge was sent to Christ's Hospital school in London, and later to Jesus College, Cambridge. He spent his summer holidays at Ottery.

Benjamin Disraeli (1804-1881)

Better remembered for his part-time job as Prime Minister, Benjamin Disraeli wrote 17 novels and a number of non-fiction titles. Perhaps the best is *Sybil, or the Two Nations.* (It was Disraeli who coined the phrase 'one-nation Tory'.) He and his wife became very friendly with a wealthy Torquay widow, Sarah Brydges Williams, who believed they were related, and they frequently stayed at her home, Mount Braddon. When she died she left the villa to Disraeli, who soon sold it.

Sir Arthur Conan Doyle (1859-1930)

Doyle was born in Edinburgh, and qualified from the University of Edinburgh Medical School. When starting out on his medical career he accepted an invitation to work with a fellow graduate, George Turnavine Budd, who had set up a practice in Plymouth. After a few weeks they had a disagreement: Doyle left to pursue his career in Portsmouth.

Later in that summer of 1882 he took a short holiday with friends: they walked from Plymouth to Tavistock where the trip was abandoned because of foul weather, but the wildness of the moor had an immediate effect on Doyle. Nearly twenty years later, on a ship returning from South Africa, he met the war correspondent Bertram Fletcher Robinson, who told Doyle legends of the Dartmoor hell-hounds, including those associated with the wicked Squire Cabell whose tomb is to be found in the old churchyard at Buckfastleigh. In 1901 they made a research trip, staying at the Duchy Hotel in Princetown, and *The Hound of the Baskervilles* was the result.

'George Eliot' a.k.a. Marian Evans and Mrs Lewes (1819-1880)

A visit to Ilfracombe in 1856 with her husband (except that he was unable to get a divorce so they weren't legally married) is recorded in her journal. As well as nature research among the rock pools, they took long walks along the quiet lanes, probably including the route we have given. Of the lanes, George Eliot wrote:

> I have talked of the Ilfracombe lanes without describing them, for to describe them one ought to know the names of all the lovely wild flowers that cluster on their banks. Almost every yard of these banks is a 'Hunt' picture – a delicious crowding of mosses and delicate trefoil, and wild strawberries, and ferns great and small. But the crowning beauty of the lanes is the springs, that gush out in little recesses by the side of the road – recesses glossy with liverwort and feathery with fern...
> I never before longed so much to know names of things as during this visit to Ilfracombe.

John Gay (1685-1732)

Quite possibly you've never hear of him, but you will have heard of his most famous work, *The Beggar's Opera*. Gay was born and educated in Barnstaple, and was apprenticed to a London silk mercer, then returned to Barnstaple. But then he went back to London, became acquainted with the great writers of his time, and made a successful literary career. He is buried in Poets' Corner, with an epitaph he composed for himself:

> Life is a jest and all things show it.
> I thought so once, and now I know it.

Charles Kingsley (1819-1875)

Charles Kingsley was born at Holne on Dartmoor in 1819. His father was vicar there, then vicar of Clovelly and later rector of Chelsea. Kingsley remained passionate about Devon, though he spent most of his life as rector of Eversley in Hampshire. He said 'I feel myself a stranger and a sojourner in a foreign land the moment I get east of Taunton Deane.' Westward Ho! in North Devon was named after his novel of that title, including the exclamation mark.

In 1855 he spent a summer at Torquay for the sake of his wife's health, and while there wrote *Glaucus, or the Wonders of the Shore*, a natural history book based on observation, and his fascination with sea life is a feature of his children's book *The Water Babies*, which is also in part a satire on the anti-Darwinists.

Rudyard Kipling (1865-1936)

Kipling was born in India, and sent by his ex-pat parents to England, where he was educated at the United Services College in Westward Ho! His novel *Stalky & Co* is a recollection of that time. From 1896 to 1898 he lived in the magnificent Rock House, Maidencombe, Torquay. He loved the surroundings, but not the other inhabitants, writing:

> We are a rummy breed – and, O Lord, the ponderous wealthy society. Torquay is such a place as I do desire to upset by dancing through it with nothing on but my spectacles.
>
> Villas, clipped hedges and shaven lawns; fat old ladies with respirators and obese landaus. The Almighty is a discursive and frivolous trifler compared with some of 'em… but the land is undeniably lovely and I am making friends with the farmers.

Dame Hilary Mantel (1952-)

One of Britain's greatest living novelists, Hilary Mantel née Thomson was born in Derbyshire, and adopted her stepfather Jack Mantel's name. She and her geologist husband have lived at times in Botswana and in Jeddah, but moved to Budleigh Salterton in 2010, where she is involved in local activities including the Literary Festival. She had first seen the town from the cliffs to its west as a teenager, and longed to live there.

Sir Walter Raleigh (1552?-1618)

Raleigh was brought up at Hayes Barton, near Budleigh Salterton. His mother's family, the Champernownes, were well connected at court, and Raleigh and his half-brothers the Gilberts benefitted greatly from that. In 1585 Raleigh was knighted, became Warden of the Stannaries and Vice-Admiral of Devon and Cornwall and was given colonialist rights. He fell out of favour with Queen Elizabeth on account of a clandestine marriage, and even more out of favour with James I, and was executed. Raleigh wrote poetry and also *A History of the World*.

William Makepeace Thackeray (1811-1863)

Thackeray was born in India, but was sent to England for his education. His mother and stepfather settled at Larkbeare, near Ottery St Mary, and he spent some time there before going to Cambridge, and again in the vacations. Ottery features as 'Clavering' and Exeter as 'Chatteris' in his comic and satirical novel *Pendennis*, some aspects of which are based on Thackeray's own experience, but fall short of being totally autobiographical. There is a quite detailed description of the town.

Henry Williamson (1895-1977)

The author of *Tarka the Otter* was a Londoner, but he moved to Georgeham, near Croyde, in 1921, when he decided to make writing his career. *Tarka* was published in 1927, and its success meant that Williamson could continue as a full time writer. However in 1936 he bought a farm in Norfolk, where he stayed till his first marriage broke down, returning to Georgeham in 1946, where he produced a novel a year, all now largely forgotten.